LEADERS OF THE WORLD
General Editor: **ROBERT MAXWELL, M.C.**

DENG XIAOPING

eeches and Writings

LEADERS OF THE WORLD
General Editor: ROBERT MAXWELL, M.C.

Other Volumes in the Series

Y. V. ANDROPOV
*General Secretary of the CPSU and
President of the Presidium of the Supreme Soviet of the USSR*

LEONID ILYICH BREZHNEV
*President of the Presidium of the Supreme Soviet of the USSR,
General Secretary of the Communist Party of the Soviet Union*

NICOLAE CEAUSESCU
*President of Romania and General Secretary of the
Romanian Communist Party*

K. V. CHERNENKO
*General Secretary of the CPSU and
President of the Presidium of the Supreme Soviet of the USSR*

MORARJI DESAI
Prime Minister of India

ERICH HONECKER
Party Leader and Head of State of the German Democratic Republic

RONALD REAGAN
President of the United States of America

TODOR ZHIVKOV
*General Secretary of the Central Committee of the Bulgarian
Communist Party and President of the State Council of the
People's Republic of Bulgaria*

Volumes in preparation

JANOS KADAR
First Secretary of the Hungarian Communist Party

FRANCOIS MITTERAND
President of the French Republic

DENG XIAOPING

DENG XIAOPING

*Chairman of the Military Commission
and of the Advisory Commission of the
Central Committee of the Communist Party of China*

Speeches and Writings

PERGAMON PRESS
OXFORD · NEW YORK · TORONTO · SYDNEY · PARIS · FRANKFURT

U.K.	Pergamon Press Ltd., Headington Hill Hall, Oxford OX3 0BW, England
U.S.A.	Pergamon Press Inc., Maxwell House, Fairview Park, Elmsford, New York 10523, U.S.A.
CANADA	Pergamon Press Canada Ltd., Suite 104, 150 Consumers Road, Willowdale, Ontario M2J 1P9, Canada
AUSTRALIA	Pergamon Press (Aust.) Pty. Ltd., P.O. Box 544, Potts Point, N.S.W. 2011, Australia
FRANCE	Pergamon Press SARL, 24 rue des Ecoles, 75240 Paris, Cedex 05, France
FEDERAL REPUBLIC OF GERMANY	Pergamon Press GmbH, Hammerweg 6, D-6242 Kronberg-Taunus, Federal Republic of Germany

Copyright © 1984 Pergamon Press Ltd.

All Rights Reserved. No part of this publication may be reproduced, stored in a retrieval system or transmitted in any form or by any means: electronic, electrostatic, magnetic tape, mechanical, photocopying, recording or otherwise, without permission in writing from the publishers.

All photographs have been provided by Xinhua News Agency and may not be reproduced without permission

First edition 1984
Reprinted 1985

Library of Congress Cataloging in Publication Data
Teng Hsiao-p'ing, 1904 -
Speeches and writings
(Leaders of the world)
Includes index.
Contents: Introduction/by Robert Maxwell — Report on the revision of the Constitution of the Communist Party of China, delivered at the Eighth National Congress of the Communist Party of China, 16 September 1956 [etc.]
I. Title.
DS778.T39A5   1984   320.5′323   84-22724

British Library Cataloguing in Publication Data
Deng Xiaoping
Speeches and writings.—(Leaders of the world)
1. China—Politics and government—1949–1976.
China—Politics and government—1976–
I. Title
951.05′8′0924   DS777.75
ISBN 0-08-028165-6 (Hardcover)
ISBN 0-08-028166-4 (Flexicover)

Printed in Great Britain by A. Wheaton & Co. Ltd., Exeter

Publisher's Note

Although Vice-Chairman Deng Xiaoping wrote his Foreword in 1981, this volume includes two speeches delivered in 1982 and 1984, and written answers to questions put to him by Robert Maxwell in 1982.

Contents

Introduction by Robert Maxwell ... ix

Foreword by Deng Xiaoping ... xi

Report on the Revision of the Constitution of the Communist Party of China delivered at the Eighth National Congress of the Communist Party of China, 16 September 1956 ... 1

Speech at the Opening Ceremony of the National Conference on Science, 18 March 1978 ... 40

Speech at the National Conference on Education, 22 April 1978 ... 54

Emancipate the Mind, Seek Truth from Facts and Unite as One in Looking to the Future, 13 December 1978 ... 62

The United Front and the Tasks of the Chinese People's Political Consultative Conference in the New Period, 15 June 1979 ... 75

Speech Greeting the Fourth Congress of Chinese Writers and Artists, 30 October 1979 ... 78

Opening Speech at the Twelfth National Congress of the CPC, 1 September 1982 ... 85

Speech Delivered at the National Day Ceremony, 1 October 1984 ... 89

Interview of Deng Xiaoping by Robert Maxwell on Current Affairs ... 91

Index ... 99

Introduction

By Robert Maxwell
General Editor of the "Leaders of the World" Series

Although Deng Xiaoping retains chairmanship of the Party and State military commissions, he has now shed the most senior posts in State and Party to make way for younger men. Nevertheless, there can be no doubt that this resilient and sturdy leader enjoys unrivalled authority over the Chinese nation of one billion citizens. He has twice reached the summit of political power, twice been plunged into obscurity, only to rise a third time to take control of his country's destiny. He has masterminded China's miraculous recovery from the chaos of the Cultural Revolution, and is among the outstanding statesmen of our time.

Pragmatism has been the hallmark of Deng's leadership. This is typified by his famous dictum: "It doesn't matter whether the cat is black or white as long as it catches mice." Deng's private remark that "you cannot eat socialism" underlines his view that the socialist state will ultimately be judged by its performance in improving the living standards of the people while increasing its capability for self-defence.

China is pursuing these aims through its policy of the "Four Modernisations": the accelerated development of agriculture, industry, science and technology, and national defence. To further these objectives, Deng has introduced the "open door" policy of encouraging foreign investment and expanding international trade, while exploiting China's enormous natural resources to acquire Western technology and develop modern production techniques. The climate of *rapprochement* with the West created by this approach has enabled Deng to achieve by peaceful means the greatest of China's "sacred tasks"—the resumption of sovereignty over Hong Kong in 1997.

Deng has expressed the hope of living to witness this triumph, of which he is the principal architect, but whatever the future holds, there can be no doubt that—at the age of 80—his achievements mark him out as an outstanding leader of his people. It is an honour to publish his works in our series.

ROBERT MAXWELL
General Editor

Oxford, November 1984

Foreword

This book, published by Pergamon Press, is a collection of some of my speeches delivered between 1956 and 1979 on political affairs, science, education, and literature and art.

From the mid-1950s through the 1970s the world has progressed amidst complex contradictions and great turmoil. Socialist China and the Chinese Communist Party have also followed an unusual path of their own. When the first speech in this collection—"Report on the Revision of the Constitution of the Communist Party of China"—was delivered at the Party's Eighth National Congress convened in 1956, China's socialist cause was attracting worldwide attention with its vigorous progress and enormous achievements in bringing about a profound change in Chinese society. But the "Cultural Revolution" (1966–76) brought catastrophe upon the Chinese people. It was a tremendous ordeal for the whole country. Since October 1976, and particularly since the Third Plenary Session of the Party's Eleventh Central Committee held in 1978, China has returned to the path of healthy development. Most of the speeches collected here belong to this latter period. Perhaps this little collection will provide some additional information to people elsewhere who are interested in Chinese affairs, in the work of the Chinese Communist Party, and in our history over the last few decades. That is why I have agreed to its publication.

Chairman Mao Zedong said: "Can a Communist, who is an internationalist, at the same time be a patriot? We hold that he not only can be, but must be." As a member of the Chinese nation, I feel honoured to be a citizen of the international community. I am a son of the Chinese people. I deeply love my motherland and her people. We Chinese have created a glorious and ancient civilization. But we have also undergone manifold sufferings and hardships and waged unremitting struggles, paying dearly for them. Today we are conscientiously summing up our experience and, in the context of stability and unity, are devoting ourselves to building a civilization which is both materially developed and socialist in spirit. Through our own creative labour, we will radically transform the backward aspects of our country so that, with an entirely new look, it will take its place in the front ranks of the nations of the world. Together with the people of other countries, we will push forward the just cause of human progress. I am firmly convinced that the future of China belongs to the people of China, and that the future of the world belongs to the people of the world.

China's recent developments in the economic, political, cultural and other spheres make me think that if I were now to address the same topics covered in these speeches, I would do so in a more comprehensive way. However, the past is the past: it cannot be changed. We can only try to arrive at a more profound understanding of it. If they lose their value some day, that will only mean that society has advanced rapidly. And what is wrong with that?

Please allow me to express my thanks to all our friends in various countries who have shown concern for China's cause and the destiny of the Chinese people.

14 February 1981   DENG XIAOPING

Report on the Revision of the Constitution of the Communist Party of China

Delivered at the Eighth National Congress of the Communist Party of China, 16 September 1956

Comrades,

More than eleven years have passed since the Seventh National Congress of our Party was held in April 1945. During this period tremendous changes have taken place both in our country and in our Party. In a little over three years, our Party, led by the Central Committee with Comrade Mao Zedong at the head and rallying the people of the whole country, defeated Chiang Kai-shek's army of several million men, overthrew the rule of imperialism, feudalism and bureaucrat-capitalism, and established the People's Republic of China. Following this nationwide victory in the revolution, the Party and the People's Government, in no more than three years, completed the rehabilitation of our national economy and carried out a series of democratic reforms. From 1953 on, the Party and the People's Government have been engaged in the construction work mapped out in the First Five-Year Plan and have won decisive victories in socialist transformation. This succession of magnificent victories furnishes indisputable proof of the correctness of the political line laid down by the Seventh Congress and of the political leadership of the Central Committee ever since. It is likewise indisputable proof of the correctness of the organizational line laid down by that Congress and of the organizational leadership of the Central Committee in the same period. Comrade Liu Shaoqi has already made a detailed report on the various aspects of the work done by the Party during this period and the tasks that now confront it. Entrusted by the Central Committee, I am making this report on the revisions in our Party Constitution, revisions necessitated by the changes that have taken place in the situation of the Party.

I

The draft of the Party Constitution now before the Congress for consideration is the product of discussions by Party organizations in all localities and of repeated revision. There is no difference in fundamental principle between the present draft and the Constitution adopted at the Seventh Congress, but many specific changes have been made in content, including a number of changes regarding principles.

At the time of the Seventh Congress, our People's Revolution had not yet achieved victory in most parts of the country. The majority of our cities and communication lines were still under the occupation of the Japanese aggressors, and the greater part of the rear areas was still under the control of the Chiang Kai-shek government. The various liberated areas under the leadership of the Party were still cut off from one another by the enemy. At that time there were 1,210,000 Party members, the vast majority of whom were in the rural districts in the liberated areas. Our Party members in the Kuomintang-controlled and Japanese-occupied areas were all working underground.

Now the situation in our country is entirely changed. Under the leadership of our Party, the People's Revolution won nationwide victory in 1949, and an unprecedented national unification was realized. Except in a few border areas, we have not only completed the tasks set for the stage of bourgeois-democratic revolution but in the main carried out the tasks for the stage of socialist revolution. Moreover, in the past seven years we have scored tremendous achievements in all spheres of our socialist construction. All this has brought about a fundamental change in China's class relationships. The working class has become the leading class in the state; the peasantry has changed from individual farming to co-operative farming; and the *bourgeoisie* as a class is on its way to extinction.

A great change has also come about in the situation of our Party. The Communist Party of China is now a party in power, playing the leading role in all the work of the state. Party organizations are found in every city and town, in every county and district, in every major enterprise and among the various nationalities. Party membership has increased ninefold since the Seventh Congress and nearly threefold since our nationwide victory in 1949. Furthermore, the majority of our Party members are now working in government offices, economic enterprises, cultural establishments and people's organizations at all levels. All these changes make it imperative for us to pay the greatest attention to strengthening the Party's organizational and educational work among the membership.

Being in a position of power, our Party has been confronted with new tests. Generally speaking, it has stood the tests of the last seven years. Our country has made remarkable progress in every sphere, and the overwhelming majority of our Party members are working hard and doing well at their posts. But the experience of these seven years has shown us that, with the Party in power, our comrades are liable to become tainted with bureaucracy. For both Party organizations and individual members, the danger of becoming divorced from reality and from the masses has increased rather than decreased. Any such alienation is bound to give rise to errors of subjectivism; that is, to errors of dogmatism and empiricism, and such errors have increased rather than decreased in our Party compared with the situation a few years ago.

The position of the Party as a party in power can also easily breed arrogance and self-complacency among the membership. After achieving the least bit of success in their work, some Party members become puffed-up, looking down upon others, upon the masses, upon non-Party personages, as if being Party members puts them head and shoulders above non-Party people. Some, fond of showing off in their role as leaders, like to order the masses about and are reluctant to consult them when problems crop up. This is in fact a tendency towards narrow sectarianism, a dangerous tendency which leads to the most serious isolation from the masses.

In view of this situation, the Party must pay constant attention to combating subjectivism, bureaucracy and sectarianism, and must always guard against the danger of becoming divorced from reality and from the masses. Therefore, apart from strengthening the ideological education of its members, the Party has an even more important task, namely, to strengthen the Party's leadership in various spheres and to make appropriate provisions in both the state and the Party systems to facilitate strict supervision over our Party organizations and Party members.

We need supervision from within the Party, and we likewise need supervision of our Party organizations and Party members by the masses and by non-Party personages. Whether supervision comes from inside or outside the Party, the crucial thing is to promote the democratic life of the Party and the state, and to carry forward our Party's traditional style of work, namely, "integrating theory with practice, forging close links with the masses and practising self-criticism", as expounded by Comrade Mao Zedong in his political report to the Seventh Congress.

It is clear that the great changes in our country and our Party mentioned above place higher rather than lower demands on our Party. Clearly too, more is expected of our Party members, not less. The draft Constitution now before the Congress contains appropriate revisions of the existing Party Constitution, made on the basis of the new conditions and demands.

Furthermore, since the Seventh Congress our Party has accumulated a great deal of fresh experience in maintaining close ties with the people and organizing them, in uniting with the democratic forces outside the Party, in guiding state affairs and economic work, and in expanding and consolidating the Party and giving leadership to all the Party organizations and the mass of the membership so that they may unite as one and do their work well. This store of new experience too finds suitable expression in the draft Constitution.

That is all I want to say regarding the conditions on the basis of which the Party Constitution has been revised.

II

The General Programme of the draft Constitution, when compared with that of the existing Constitution, will be found to contain many changes, especially on the political side. This is readily understandable. The General Programme in our Party Constitution embodies the basic political and organizational programme of the Party. Now that a fundamental change has taken place in the country's political situation, fundamental changes must accordingly be made in our political programme for the present period. With regard to the political section of the General Programme, I think no further explanation is needed, for you have heard Comrade Liu Shaoqi's report. What does require elaboration regarding the General Programme of the draft Constitution is first of all the question of the Party's mass line.

The question of the mass line is not a new one in Party work. The Party Constitution adopted by the Seventh Congress, and particularly its General Programme, is permeated with the spirit of the mass line. At that Congress, illuminating explanations of the mass line were given by Comrade Mao Zedong in his political report when he spoke about the Party's style of work, and also by Comrade Liu Shaoqi when he dealt with the General Programme in his report on the revision of the Party Constitution. The reasons for again emphasizing and explaining it are as follows. First, the mass line is a fundamental question in the Party's organizational work and in the Party Constitution and therefore needs constant reiteration in Party education. True, this question was explained at the Seventh Congress, but since the vast majority of our present members have joined the Party since the last Congress, and since practice has shown that many comrades have failed to adhere consistently to the mass line, it is clear that education on the mass line within the Party can by no means be considered adequate. Secondly, the experience gained by the Party in the eleven years of actual struggle since the last Congress has given the mass line a richer and deeper content, and it has therefore been further elucidated in the draft Party Constitution. The General Programme in the draft stresses that the Party must unceasingly strive to carry forward the tradition of the mass line in Party work and points out that since the Party is now in power, this task has acquired even greater significance than before.

What is the mass line in Party work? Briefly stated, it has two aspects. On the one hand, it recognizes that the people must liberate themselves, that the Party's entire task is to serve the people heart and soul, and that the Party's role in leading the masses lies in pointing out to them the correct path of struggle and in helping them to strive for and build a happy life through their own efforts. Consequently, the Party must keep in close contact with the masses and rely on them, and must under no circumstances lose touch with them or place itself above them. For the same reason every Party member must cultivate the style of work which stresses serving the people, holding himself responsible to them, never failing to consult them and being ever ready to share their joys and sorrows.

On the other hand, the mass line recognizes that the Party's ability to go on exercising correct leadership hinges upon its ability to apply the method of "from the masses and to the masses". This means—to quote from the Central Committee's "Resolution on Methods of Leadership", drafted by Comrade Mao Zedong—"take the ideas of the masses (scattered and unsystematic ideas) and concentrate them (through study turn them into concentrated and systematic ideas), then go to the masses and propagate and explain these ideas until the masses embrace them as their own, hold fast to them and translate them into action, and test the correctness of these ideas in such action. Then once again concentrate ideas from the masses and once again go to the masses so that the ideas are persevered in and carried through. And so on, over and over again in an endless spiral, with the ideas becoming more correct, more vital and richer each time."

The mass line in Party work is of profound theoretical and practical significance. Marxism has always recognized that history, in the final analysis, is made by the people. Only by relying on its own mass strength and that of all labouring people will the working class be able to fulfil its historical mission—the mission of liberating itself and, at the same time, all labouring people. The higher the level of consciousness, enthusiasm and creativity of the masses, the more flourishing the cause of the working class. Consequently, a political party of the working class, unlike the political parties of the *bourgeoisie*, never regards the masses as its tools, but consciously regards itself as their tool for carrying out their given historical mission in a specific historical period. The Communist Party is the collective body of the advanced elements among the working class and the labouring people, and there can be no doubt as to its great role in leading the masses. But the Party can play its part as vanguard and lead the masses forward precisely and solely because it whole-heartedly serves the masses, represents their will and interests, and strives to help them organize themselves to fight for their own interests and for the fulfilment of their own will. To affirm this concept of the Party is to affirm that the Party has no right whatever to place itself above the masses, that is, it has no right to act towards the masses as if it were dispensing favours, to take everything into its own hands and impose its will "by decree"—to affirm that it has no right to lord it over the people.

Unless we understand from a correct approach to knowledge that our Party's policies must of necessity undergo the process of "coming from the masses and going back to the masses", we cannot arrive at a real solution to the problem of the Party's relations with the masses. Practice has shown that there are many people who, while not lacking the desire to serve the masses, bungle their work in a way that does great harm to the masses. This is because they think that, being advanced elements, or being leaders, they know a great deal more than the masses. Therefore, they neither learn from the masses nor consult them, with the result that their ideas more often than not prove impracticable. Instead of learning from their mistakes and failures, they blame them on the backwardness of the masses or some incidental factor, and, abusing the Party's prestige, they arbitrarily cling to their own course, thereby aggravating their mistakes and failures. In the history of our Party such subjectivists have caused incalculable losses to the Party, to the Chinese revolution and to the Chinese people. They do not understand that only those who really know how to be pupils of the masses can ever become their teachers and that only by continuing to be pupils can they continue to be teachers. A party and its members can point out the correct path and lead the masses forward only by carefully summing up the experience and pooling their wisdom. We do not tail behind the masses, and we know quite well that the opinions which come from the masses cannot all be correct and mature. What we mean by summing up the experience of the masses and pooling their wisdom is by no means a simple process of accumulation; there must be classification, analysis, critical judgement and synthesis. But without investigation and study of the experience and opinions of the masses, no leader, however talented, can lead correctly. Mistakes may still arise even after classification, analysis, critical judgement and synthesis. But by constantly consulting the masses and studying their practice, the Party will be able to make fewer mistakes and to discover and correct them in time to prevent them from becoming serious.

The mass line in Party work, therefore, demands that Party leaders should conduct themselves with modesty and prudence. Arrogance, arbitrariness, rashness, assertion of one's own cleverness, failure to consult the masses, the forcing of one's opinions on others, and persistence in errors to maintain one's own prestige—all these are utterly incompatible with the Party's mass line.

Let us look back on the path our Party has traversed since the Seventh Congress through the War of Liberation (1946–9), the land reform and the elimination of counter-revolutionaries, the socialist transformation of agriculture, handicrafts and capitalist industry and commerce, and the development of industry, agriculture and other economic and cultural work—in all these fields our Party has won great victories. But which of them could have been won without following the mass line? For example, why is it that the officers and men of the People's Liberation Army could defeat the Kuomintang army, which was superior both in numbers and in equipment? Is it not chiefly because they upheld the principle of serving the people, built up exemplary relations between the army and the people through their self-sacrificing behaviour, created inside the armed forces a comradeship which gave full play to the initiative of junior officers and the rank and file, and drew conclusions from the experience of each battle by depending on them, thus making continual strategic and tactical progress? Soldiers carrying water for local inhabitants, officers covering sleeping soldiers with blankets, the calling of "collective wisdom meetings" in trenches, caring for the health and self-respect of the captured and not searching their pockets—all these appear to be trivial matters, but they had a good deal to do with the winning of many a great victory.

Again, why is it that hundreds of millions of peasants, oppressed by the landlords for thousands of years, have become masters of their own fate and are resolved to build up a new life of their own? Is it not because in the period of the land reform our Party sent out work teams which really went among the poor peasants, discovered the active elements among them, aroused their class consciousness, mobilized the peasants themselves to overthrow the rule of the landlords and share out their land, and thus helped the peasants really to recognize their own strength and form their own leading nuclei, and which didn't just turn the landlords' land over to the peasants by issuing government orders? What has made the peasants join the agricultural producers' co-operatives so readily and of their own will? Is it not because our Party, proceeding from the experience of the masses themselves, gave extensive assistance to the peasants in organizing seasonal mutual-aid teams, then year-round mutual-aid teams, then elementary co-operatives, and finally advanced co-operatives, so that the peasants might, through practice, come to a firm belief in the superiority of co-operation?

Let me give another example. How is it that our country has been able to achieve so much with a minimum of mistakes in the campaign for combing out counter-revolutionaries? Is it not because we adopted the correct policy of co-ordinating the work of relevant government departments with the mobilization of the masses? Is it not because we fully mobilized the masses that, under the sharp and watchful eyes of hundreds of millions of people, a large number of counter-revolutionaries, unable to find hiding-places, have been forced to bow their heads, admit their guilt, and embrace the opportunity to reform themselves and turn over a new leaf?

Yet another example. In less than three years after the liberation of the whole country, we changed the appallingly corrupt social conventions of the old society into new social conventions imbued with a fine ethical character. How could such results have been obtained without conscious and voluntary participation, without mutual education, mutual persuasion and help on the part of the masses?

We might also ask: Could we have completely wiped out the evil of opium-smoking and won victories in our large-scale patriotic public health movement, in production, construction, and so on—could we have won any one of these victories if the movement or the tasks in question had not actually reflected the demands of the broad masses and been translated into conscious and voluntary action by them?

When we speak of the great victories our Party has won as a result of following the mass line, we certainly do not mean that all our work in this regard has been excellent. On the contrary, our purpose is to remind the whole Party that if correct application of the mass line has brought success, any departure from it will surely damage our work and the people's interests. As I have already said, the present position of our Party as a party in power throughout the country has greatly increased the danger of our becoming divorced from the masses, and the damage this may do to the masses is also greater than before. That is why it is of special significance at present to seriously propagate and carry out the mass line throughout the Party.

Various tendencies towards bureaucracy are springing up among many functionaries in Party organizations and state organs. Not a few leading bodies and leading cadres hold themselves aloof and do not try to get close to the masses; they pay no special attention to investigation and study and are unaware of how things really stand in their work. When they consider their tasks and make decisions they very often start, not from the objective conditions and what the masses are actually doing, but subjectively from inaccurate information or from their own imagination and wishes. Therefore, although they issue numerous resolutions and instructions, some are not strictly correct and others are even entirely wrong. When they carry out the instructions of higher organizations and the Central

Committee, they often fail to consult their subordinate comrades and the masses and to take the actual conditions of a given time and place into consideration but just follow these instructions mechanically and blindly. They often feel satisfied with superficial achievements and ignore the actual results of their work. They see only its positive side and not the negative side, or else they go after quantity alone and do not care much about quality. They have no definite ideas about their work, so they constantly vacillate, now falling victim to Rightist conservatism with their ideas lagging behind reality, now rashly placing undue emphasis on quantity and speed, attempting to go beyond what is actually possible.

Not a few responsible comrades in different departments spend most of their time dealing with official papers and telegrams and attending too many unnecessary meetings. They seldom go deep into the basic organizations and into the midst of the masses in order to find out their needs and study their experience, and thus they inevitably slip into routine and red tape. Not a few leading comrades like to turn their own departments into huge structures. With these unwieldy and overlapping structures, they are setting up many artificial barriers between themselves and the masses, so that the opinions and needs of the masses cannot be accurately and promptly brought to their notice, nor can their own decisions and instructions be correctly and quickly conveyed to the masses. When problems calling for immediate solution arise, quite a number of responsible comrades do not pitch in and tackle them, but pass them on to those on a lower rung of the departmental ladder, who in turn pass them on to others on a still lower rung; eventually the solution of the problem is reported again from rung to rung by the reverse process. In consequence, the problems are either mishandled or left unsolved until too late. In either case, work is bound to suffer. What is even more serious is that some leading comrades are unwilling to come into contact with the masses and do not feel any concern for their welfare; instead of trying actively to solve the problems for which the masses want an immediate solution, they remain aloof and indifferent.

Among some cadres bureaucracy assumes the form of swollen conceit and self-complacency. These comrades exaggerate the role of the individual and emphasize personal prestige. They lend a willing ear to flattery and praise but cannot bear criticism or supervision; some bad characters go so far as to stifle criticism and resort to reprisals against their critics. There are people of yet another kind in our Party who turn the relations between the Party and the people upside down. Far from serving the people, they abuse their authority over the people and do all manner of evil things in contravention of law and discipline. This is a vicious, anti-popular style of work, a manifestation in our own ranks of the working style characteristic of the old ruling classes. Although the number of such cadres is small, the harm they do is serious.

Another fairly widespread form of bureaucracy is commandism. Quite a number of Party organizations and cadres fail to consult the masses before they make decisions and issue instructions. Moreover, in the process of implementing these decisions and instructions they do not try to persuade and educate the masses, but simply resort to issuing orders to get things done. Comrades who make these mistakes may subjectively wish to do things well, but in fact they do their work very badly. Such mistakes of commandism are found more glaring among the primary Party organizations and their cadres, but in the lower organizations they are often inseparable from the subjectivist and bureaucratic methods of leadership of the leading bodies above them.

The existence of the mistakes I have mentioned shows that the mass line is still far from being thoroughly carried out in our Party. We must constantly combat such manifestations of bureaucracy and isolation from the masses. But we must also realize that bureaucracy is a historical survival of the age-long rule of exploiters and has a deep and far-reaching influence on socio-political life. Hence, to carry out the mass line and overcome bureaucracy necessarily involves a long-term struggle.

This task is set forth both in the General Programme and in all the relevant articles of the draft Party Constitution. Of course, these provisions by themselves cannot solve the problem. We must moreover adopt a series of practical measures. What measures must we take?

First, we must vigorously expound the mass line throughout the Party's educational network, in the educational literature for Party members and in all Party newspapers and periodicals.

Secondly, we must systematically improve the working methods of leading bodies at all levels so that leading personnel will have ample time to go deep among the masses and become good at studying their conditions, their experience and their opinions by investigating typical situations. This should replace the present practice of spending most of the time in offices, going over papers and documents and holding meetings inside the leading bodies. The staffs of leading bodies should be cut down and the number of organizational levels reduced. The leading bodies should send as many of their superfluous personnel as possible to lower bodies and have the remaining ones handle practical work themselves, as a means of guarding against the danger of the leading bodies turning bureaucratic.

Thirdly, we must see to it that the democratic life of the Party and the state is fully developed so that the lower organizations of the Party and government will have adequate opportunities and guarantees for making timely and fearless criticism of the mistakes and shortcomings found in the work of the higher bodies. And we must ensure that all kinds of Party or state conferences, especially the Party congresses and people's congresses at all levels, serve as forums where the opinions of the masses can be fully voiced and criticism and debate unfolded.

Fourthly, we must strengthen supervision by the Party and the state, so as to discover and promptly correct all kinds of bureaucratic practices, and adopt due and prompt disciplinary measures against those who have contravened law and discipline or seriously damaged the interests of the masses.

Fifthly, the Party organizations in all localities and departments must draw on the experience gained in past Party rectification campaigns and check up on the working style of all Party members at regular intervals, adopting the methods of criticism by the masses and self-criticism. In particular, they must carefully check up on how the mass line is being carried out.

In the struggle to carry out the mass line and combat bureaucracy, it is of vital importance to co-operate still more closely with non-Party people and to draw as many of them as possible into the struggle. At present, however, there are a good many comrades in our Party, including some in fairly responsible positions, who still have trouble co-operating with non-Party people, being either reluctant to do so or unaccustomed to it. In fact, this is a very harmful sectarian tendency, a tendency which must be overcome if the Party's united front policy is to be thoroughly carried out.

Such comrades must be made to understand that our Party's co-operation with democratic parties and with democratic personages having no party affiliation is a long-term one and that this policy was fixed long ago. Ever since the War of Resistance Against Japan (1937–45), our Party has been pursuing a policy of co-operation with democratic personages outside the Party. And since the founding of the People's Republic of China, our co-operation with democratic parties and democratic personages without party affiliation has gone further. The experience of the last ten years or so has shown that this kind of co-operation is beneficial, and not harmful, to the cause of our Party. Many of the democratic personages who co-operated with us were at first political representatives of the *bourgeoisie* or the petty *bourgeoisie*, but in the course of co-operation they have gradually and in varying degrees shifted their standpoint towards socialism and will continue to do so. Of course, there are struggles in this kind of co-operation. This is inevitable. But the point is that these democratic personages can provide a kind of supervision over our Party which cannot easily be provided by Party members alone; they can discover mistakes and shortcomings in our work which may escape our own notice and can render us valuable help. The help they can give us is bound to increase now that socialist transformation has won a decisive victory, and their standpoint is coming closer to ours than before. Therefore, our task is to continue to broaden our co-operation with non-Party people and to enable them to play an even greater role in our struggle against bureaucracy and in all aspects of state affairs.

That is all I want to say about the significance of the mass line and the need for the Party to persist in it in its work.

III

Democratic centralism is our Party's Leninist organizational principle. It is the fundamental organizational principle of the Party, the mass line in Party work applied to all activities inside the Party itself. In the General Programme and in Chapter Two of the draft Constitution, more detailed provisions are made concerning democratic centralism inside the Party. These provisions are the result of many years' experience gained in the organizational life of our Party.

The Party depends on all its members and organizations to maintain contact with the masses. The collection of opinions and experience from among the masses, the publicizing of Party policies so as to turn them into the views of the masses themselves, and the organization of the masses to put these policies into effect—all this must be done, generally speaking, through the efforts of the Party members and lower-level Party organizations. Therefore, the correct regulation of relations between the Party organization and its members, between higher and lower Party organizations and between central and local Party organizations is of special significance to the question of democratic centralism inside the Party.

In the history of our Party, deviations occurred in the relations between higher and lower organizations. During the period when "Left" opportunism was dominant in the Party, the deviation took the form of excessive centralization. The lower organizations then had practically no right to voice their opinions to the higher organizations. The leaders in the higher organizations not only showed no interest in the situation and opinions of the lower organizations but even attacked those people who, basing themselves on the actual situation, put forward reasoned opinions which differed from those of the higher organizations. This kind of mistake was overcome, in the main, after the Central Committee brought the domination of "Left" opportunism to an end in January 1935.

Since 1935 the relations between higher and lower organizations and between central and local organizations in our Party have been normal on the whole. When tackling major issues of a national character, the Central

Committee has always done its best to consult the comrades working in the various localities and departments and to listen to their opinions; as a general rule, free and repeated discussions have taken place when there were differences of opinion. As we all know, many important directives of the Central Committee are first sent out in draft form to local organizations, which are asked to suggest revisions after they have dicussed the directives and conducted trial operations; they are issued in official form only after being revised in the light of the opinions received—a process which takes several months, sometimes even more than a year, to complete. The Central Committee has also permitted local organizations to modify its directives according to local conditions if they really find it impossible to carry them out as they stand. Not only during the War of Resistance Against Japan and the War of Liberation but also in the first few years after the founding of the People's Republic, the Central Committee gave local organizations extensive powers to deal with problems independently, and facts have proved that it was perfectly correct to do so. Generally speaking, relations between higher and lower organization in all localities and departments have been governed by the same principle; the local and lower organizations respect the leadership of the Central Committee and the higher organizations, and consequently our policies have in the main been successfully carried out throughout the Party.

But during this period another kind of deviation existed inside the Party, namely, decentralism. It often happened that there were Party cadres who liked to make their particular departments into little worlds of their own. They liked to act according to their own ideas on political questions, disliked the Party's direction and supervision, and did not respect the decisions of higher organizations and the Central Committee. They did not ask for prior instructions from higher organizations and the Central Committee even on important questions that really needed uniform decisions by the Central Committee, nor did they submit reports to them later. Thus they acted contrary to Party policy and Party discipline and impaired the unity of the Party. The Central Committee has waged resolute and continual struggles against this kind of deviation. The *Decision to Strengthen the Party Spirit* (1941), the *Decision on Unifying Leadership in the Anti-Japanese Base Areas* (1942), the *Directives for Setting Up a System of Applying for Instructions and Submitting Reports and for Strengthening the Sense of Organization and Discipline* (1948), and the *Decision on Strengthening the Party Committee System* (1948)—all these documents issued by the Central Committee were designed mainly to overcome this tendency towards decentralism. The Fourth Plenary Session of the Seventh Central Committee held in February 1954 dealt another smashing blow at the errors of decentralism ideologically, politically and organizationally. Since then remnants of this deviation have been limited to certain isolated cases.

At present, the main shortcoming in the relations between higher and lower Party organizations as a whole is still that insufficient attention has been paid to encouraging the initiative and creative ability of the lower organizations. Undue emphasis on centralization manifests itself not only in the economic, cultural and other administrative work of the state, but also in Party work. Too many rigid regulations are laid down by the higher organizations, and quite a few are formulated without a careful study of the conditions and experiences of the lower organizations, with the result that the latter encounter difficulties in trying to carry them out. Many higher organizations are not yet good at getting right down to the rank and file, listening to the opinions of the lower organizations and the masses, and solving problems through consultation with the lower organizations. They are still prone to issue orders from their offices or to try to run the lower organizations themselves. Moreover, some leading functionaries at the higher levels like to put on airs and make a great show of authority. They are wont to lecture and criticize people, but are unwilling to solicit advice or listen to criticism from the lower ranks, or make any self-criticism in the presence of those working under them. Such cases, though not widespread, are by no means isolated. Unless we pay attention to this state of affairs and bring about a change, there will be no real democratic centralism in places where such a situation exists.

In the light of the different kinds of experience already mentioned, the draft Constitution makes the following additional provisions in regard to the relationship between higher and lower organizations under democratic centralism:

First, with regard to the basic requirements of democratic centralism, the following provisions are added: "All leading bodies of the Party must pay heed to the views of their lower organizations and the rank-and-file Party members, study their experiences and give prompt help in solving their problems." "Lower Party organizations must present periodical reports on their work to the Party organizations above them and ask in good time for instructions on questions which need decision by higher Party organizations."

Secondly, concerning the functions and powers of the central and local organizations and of the higher and lower Party organizations, the following article is added: "The functions and powers of the central Party organizations and those of the local Party organizations shall be appropriately divided. All questions of a national character or questions that require a uniform decision for the whole country shall be handled by the central Party organizations so as to contribute to the centralism and unity of the Party. All questions of a local character or questions that need to be decided locally shall be handled by the local Party organizations so as to find solutions appropriate to the local conditions. The functions and powers of higher and lower local Party organizations shall be appropriately divided according to the same principle."

Thirdly, with regard to discussions on questions of policy and the carrying out of decisions, the following article is added: "Before decisions on Party policy are made by the leading bodies of the Party, lower Party organizations and members of the Party committees may hold free and practical discussions inside the Party organizations and at Party meetings and submit their proposals to the leading bodies of the Party. However, once a decision is taken by the leading bodies of the Party, it must be accepted. Should a lower Party organization find that a decision made by a higher Party organization does not suit the actual conditions in its locality or in its particular department, it should request the higher Party organization concerned to modify the decision. If the higher Party organization still upholds its decision, then the lower Party organization must carry it out unconditionally."

Another fundamental question with regard to democratic centralism inside the Party is the question of collective leadership in Party organizations at all levels. Leninism requires of the Party that all decisions on important questions should be made by an appropriate collective body, and not by any individual. The Twentieth Congress of the Communist Party of the Soviet Union has thrown a searching light on the profound significance of adhering to the principle of collective leadership and combating the cult of personality, and this illuminating lesson has produced a tremendous effect on the Communist Parties of all other countries of the world as well as on the Communist Party of the Soviet Union. It is obvious that the making of decisions on important questions by individuals runs counter to the Party-building principles of political parties dedicated to the cause of communism and is bound to lead to errors. Only collective leadership which keeps in close touch with the masses conforms to the Party's principle of democratic centralism and is capable of reducing the possibility of errors to a minimum.

For a long time the tradition of our Party has been that decisions on important questions are made by a collective of the Party, and not by any individual. Although violations of the principle of collective leadership occurred in our Party from time to time, once discovered they were criticized and corrected by the Central Committee of the Party. The decision by the Central Committee in September 1948 on strengthening the Party committee system played an especially great role in strengthening collective leadership in the Party. I think it is still useful to refer to it here for the benefit of the whole Party. The decision reads:

The Party committee system is an important Party institution for ensuring collective leadership and preventing any individual from monopolizing the conduct of affairs. It has recently been found that in some (of course not all) leading bodies it is the habitual practice for one individual to monopolize the conduct of affairs and decide important problems. Solutions to important problems are decided not by Party committee meetings but by one individual, and membership in the Party committee has become nominal. Differences of opinion among committee members cannot be resolved and are left unresolved for a long time. Members of the Party committee maintain only formal, not real, unity among themselves.

This situation must be changed. From now on, a sound system of Party committee meetings must be instituted in all leading bodies, from the bureaus of the Central Committee to the prefectural Party committees, from the Party committees of the fronts to the Party committees of brigades and military areas (sub-commissions of the Revolutionary Military Commission or leading groups), and in the leading Party members' groups in government bodies, people's organizations, the news agency and the newspaper offices. All important problems (of course, not unimportant or trivial problems, or problems whose solutions have already been decided after discussion at meetings and need only be carried out) must be submitted to the committee for discussion, and the committee members present should express their views fully and reach definite decisions which should then be carried out by the members concerned. The same procedure should be followed by Party committees below the prefectural and brigade levels. In the higher leading bodies there should also be meetings of the leading cadres in the departments (for example, the propaganda department and the organizational department), commissions (for example, the labour, women's and youth commissions), schools (for example, Party schools) and offices (for example, research offices).

Of course, we must see to it that the meetings are not too long or too frequent and they must not get bogged down in discussion of petty matters lest the work be hindered. On important problems which are complicated and on which opinions differ, there must, in addition, be personal consultations before the meeting to enable the members to think things over, lest decisions by the meeting become a mere formality or no decision can be reached. Party committee meetings must be divided into two categories, standing committee meetings and plenary sessions, and the two should not be confused. Furthermore, we must take care that collective leadership is not overemphasized to the neglect of personal responsibility or vice versa. In the army, the person in command has the right to make emergency decisions during battle and when circumstances require.

This decision was implemented throughout the Party and it still holds good.

Of course the system of collective leadership had been in existence long before this decision was made. The significance of the decision lies in the fact that it summed up the Party's successful experience in the thoroughgoing practice of collective leadership, that it urged those organizations whose collective leadership was only nominal to rectify their mistakes and that it extended the scope of application of collective leadership.

As was shown by the decision, the system of collective leadership by Party committees, or to be more exact, the system of division of labour with individual responsibility among the commanders and chiefs under the collective leadership of the Party committee, had long been practised in the Chinese People's Liberation Army. It was proved by long years of wartime experience in the Chinese People's Liberation Army that this system was conducive to army work and not at all a hindrance to the direction of military operations. In the light of the experience gained over the last few years, the Central Committee has decided to have all enterprises carry out the system of collective leadership by Party committees too, i.e. the system of the personal responsibility of the factory director or manager under the collective leadership of the Party committee.

However, many shortcomings are found in the application of the system of collective leadership in our Party. In a small number of Party committees some responsible comrades are still prone to exercise exclusive personal control. They seldom call the necessary regular meetings, or, when they do call Party committee meetings, they reduce them to a mere formality. They neither give the participants a chance to prepare themselves beforehand for the questions on which decisions are going to be made, nor create an atmosphere conducive to free discussion at the meeting; hence decisions are virtually imposed on the members. This arbitrary practice by individuals under the guise of collective leadership must be firmly combated. All questions submitted to the meeting must be discussed and differences of opinion must be permitted. If in the course of discussion a serious difference of opinion arises, the discussion should be suitably prolonged and views exchanged between individuals so as to reach a real agreement among the great majority, provided the difference does not relate to an urgent matter that calls for immediate settlement. In such cases, things should not be put to the vote in a hurry, nor should any conclusion be peremptorily drawn. Similarly, when an election takes place in a Party organization, the necessary exchange of views and discussion should be conducted among the electors regarding the list of candidates put forward. Only thus can democratic life within the Party really be ensured.

Another shortcoming pointed out by the Central Committee in its decision of September 1948 still exists in many organizations. This is that too many meetings are held and that the meetings go on for too long. This not only takes up time which full-time Party workers ought to spend in getting into close contact with the masses and exercising practical leadership, thus encouraging bureaucracy and red tape, but also affects the hours of work and leisure of many Party members and non-Party people. This shortcoming is due to a lack of planning, preparation and leadership for meetings. It is also due to the misuse of meetings for bringing up a great many questions which do not need to be discussed there. This shortcoming should also be resolutely overcome.

One of the basic requirements of democratic centralism inside the Party is that Party congresses at the various levels should be held at regular intervals and should play their part to the full. More than eleven years have elapsed between the Seventh and Eighth Party Congresses. The interval was of course much too long. As to local Party congresses and conferences of Party representatives at various levels, a few localities and units have kept strictly to the provisions of the Party Constitution, but the majority have held congresses and conferences of Party representatives less often than stipulated. This is a major defect in the democratic life of our Party.

Inner-Party democracy has not been seriously affected by the long and irregular intervals between Party congresses and conferences of Party representatives. This is because in the years since the Seventh Congress a great number of cadres' conferences have been held by both the central and local organizations of the Party. These conferences, in which the Party's policies and various problems in work were discussed in a fully democratic spirit, have to a considerable extent played the role of conferences of Party representatives and even Party congresses. For example, since 1949 the Central Committee has called many conferences that were national in scope. They were: the Second (Enlarged) Plenary Session of the Seventh Central Committee, 5–13 March 1949; the Third (Enlarged) Plenary Session of the Seventh Central Committee, 6–9 June 1950; the National Conference on Financial and Economic Work, 13 June–11 August 1953; the National Conference on the State Monopoly of the Purchase and Marketing of Grain, 10–12 October 1953; the Fourth (Enlarged) Plenary Session of the Seventh Central Committee, 6–10 February 1954; the National Conference of Party Representatives, 21–31 March 1955; the Conference of Secretaries of Provincial and Municipal Party Committees, 31 July–1 August 1955; the Sixth (Enlarged) Plenary Session of the Seventh Central Committee, 4–11 October 1955; the Conference on the Transformation of Capitalist Industry and Commerce, 16–24 November 1955; the Conference on the Question of Intellectuals, 14–20 January 1956; and the Conference of Secretaries of Provincial and Municipal Party Committees, 25–28 April 1956. In general, attendance at these conferences numbered from a hundred-odd or a few hundred to over a thousand. To all intents and purposes these conferences played the role of national conferences and solved important problems in Party policy and work through free and practical discussion. Nevertheless, the holding of these conferences cannot legally replace the holding of Party congresses, or make up for the defect of not holding Party congresses regularly.

In order to completely eliminate this defect and enhance democratic life inside the Party, the Central Committee has decided to introduce a fundamental reform in the draft Party Constitution. The National Party Congress and the congresses at provincial and county levels are to be changed to a system of fixed terms, somewhat similar to that of the people's congresses at various levels. The draft Party Constitution stipulates that the National Party Congress is to be elected for a term of five years, congresses at the provincial level for three years, and congresses at the county level for two years. The congresses at all the three levels are to be called in session once a year, and consequently, as a system, the original conferences of Party representatives at the various levels will no longer be necessary. The system of Party congresses with fixed terms will greatly reduce the burden of electing delegates. The congresses may be convened at any time during their term of office. And as there will be sessions once a year, the occasions need not be elaborate affairs. The greatest merit of the system of fixed terms for the congresses lies in the fact that the congresses will thus serve as the Party's highest policy-making and supervisory organs and operate in a most effective way; this is scarcely attainable under the existing system in which congresses are held once in several years, with delegates elected afresh each time. Under the new system, the Party's most important decisions can all be brought before the congresses for discussion. The Central Committee and the provincial and county committees must submit annual reports to their respective congresses, listen to their criticisms and answer their questions. And since the delegates are elected for a fixed term and are responsible to their constituencies, they will be in a better position to regularly bring together the views and experiences of the lower organizations, of rank-and-file Party members and of the masses of the people. In this way, they will attend the sessions with a more representative character, and during the intervals when the congresses are not in session they can also exercise supervision in such forms as are appropriate over the work of the Party organs. For these reasons, we feel sure that this reform will greatly help to develop inner-Party democracy.

It must be emphasized that the Party is a militant organization. Without a centralized and unified command it would be impossible to win battles. The measures taken for the development of inner-Party democracy are not meant to weaken the necessary centralization in the Party, but to provide it with a powerful and vigorous base. This is perfectly clear to every one of us. Our purpose in proposing to improve the system of multi-level congresses is to make it easier for the Party committees to gather the opinions of the masses and to work more correctly and more effectively. Our purpose in proposing to improve the working relationship between the central and the local and between the higher and lower bodies is to enable the central and higher bodies to exercise their leadership in closer conformity with actual conditions, to concentrate their attention on work that needs to be centralized, and to strengthen their inspection and guidance of the work of the local organizations and the lower bodies. We do not advocate the strengthening of collective leadership in order to reduce the role of the individual. On the contrary, the role of the individual can only be correctly developed through the collective, while collective leadership must be combined with individual responsibility. Without division of labour and individual responsibility we would not be able to carry out any complicated work and would find ourselves in the woeful predicament of no one taking responsibility for any particular task. Whatever the organization, we need not only individual responsibility under a division of labour, but also somebody to assume overall responsibility. Aren't we all well aware that even a small group cannot function without a leader?

Here I should like to say a few words about the role of the leader in the Party. While recognizing that history is made by the people, Marxism never denies the role that outstanding individuals play in history; Marxism only points out that, in the final analysis, the role of the individual is dependent upon given social conditions. Likewise, Marxism never denies the role of leaders in political parties. In Lenin's famous words, the leaders are those who are "the most authoritative, influential and experienced". Without a doubt, their authority, their influence and their experience constitute valuable assets to the Party, the class and the people. We Chinese Communists can fully appreciate this from our own experiences. Of course, such leaders emerge naturally from the midst of the mass struggles and cannot be self-appointed. Unlike the leaders of the exploiting classes in the past, the leaders of the working-class party do not stand above the masses, but in their midst, nor above the Party, but within it. For this very reason, they must set an example in maintaining close contact with the masses, in obeying the Party organizations and in observing Party discipline. Love for the leader is essentially an expression of love for the interests of the Party, the class and the people, and not the deification of an individual. One important achievement of the Twentieth Congress of the Communist Party of the Soviet Union is that it showed us what serious consequences can follow from the deification of the individual. Our Party has always held that no political party and no individual is free from flaws and mistakes in their activities, and this has now been written into the General Programme of the draft Constitution of our Party. For the same reason, our Party abhors the deification of the individual. At the Second Plenary Session of the Seventh Central Committee held in March 1949—that is, on the eve of nationwide victory in the People's Revolution—the Central Committee, at the suggestion of Comrade Mao Zedong, took a decision prohibiting birthday celebrations for Party leaders and the use of Party leaders' names to designate places, streets and enterprises. This has had a wholesome effect in checking the glorification and exaltation of individuals. The Central Committee has always been against sending messages of greetings or telegrams reporting successes in work to the leaders. Likewise, it has been against exaggerating the role of leaders in works of art and literature. Of course the cult of personality is a social phenomenon with a long history, and it cannot but find certain reflections in our Party and public life. It is our task to continue to observe faithfully the Central Committee's principle of opposition to the elevation and glorification of the individual and to achieve a genuine consolidation of the ties between the leaders and the masses so that the Party's principle of democracy and its mass line are carried out to the full in every field.

IV

Part of the General Programme of the draft Constitution dwells on the solidarity and unity of the Party. Solidarity and unity are one of the most important questions in Party building. As the General Programme points out, "Solidarity and unity are the very life of the Party, the source of its strength. It is the sacred duty of every Party member to pay constant attention to the safeguarding of the solidarity of the Party and the consolidation of its unity."

What was the reason for the success of the People's Revolution led by our Party? First of all, of course, it was because our Party had a correct policy which represented the interests of the people. But with a correct policy alone, we could not have defeated so powerful an enemy and won victory. Our Party also kept in close touch with the people and, moreover, organized them into a united force. But if our Party itself had not been united, how could it have rallied the people?

Again, after our victorious People's Revolution, we succeeded in overcoming tremendous difficulties and obstacles, rapidly achieved the unity of the nation, quickly rehabilitated and developed our national economy, embarked on the socialist transformation of the economy and in the main completed it. On what did we depend for all this? Without the unity of our Party we could not have led the people and accomplished these complicated tasks in such a short period—this is beyond the shadow of a doubt.

Our Party has now assumed the leading role in all fields of state affairs and public activities. It is obvious that our Party as it stands is exercising a more direct and broader influence on the national life than ever before. It is to the advantage not only of the Party but also of the entire people that we should safeguard the solidarity of the Party and strengthen its unity.

The Party is the highest form of class organization. It is particularly important to point this out today when our Party has assumed the leading role in state affairs. Of course this does not mean that the Party can exercise direct command over the work of state organs or discuss questions of a purely administrative nature within the Party, overstepping the necessary line of demarcation between Party work and the work of state organs. It means, first, that Party members in state organs and particularly members of the leading Party groups formed by those in responsible positions in such organs should follow the Party's unified leadership. Secondly, the Party must regularly discuss and settle questions regarding guiding principles and policies in state affairs as well as important organizational matters, and the leading Party members' groups in state organs must see to it that these decisions are put into effect with the harmonious co-operation of non-Party personages. Thirdly, the Party must conscientiously and systematically look into the problems and work of the state organs so as to be able to put forward correct proposals which are practical and specific or to make timely revisions in the light of actual practice, and must exercise constant supervision over the work of these organs. Some comrades working in government departments do not respect the leadership of the Party, excusing themselves on the pretext that their work is of an exceptional nature, and they attempt to turn their departments into "independent kingdoms". This is a dangerous tendency which must be overcome. At the same time, some Party organizations irrationally interfere with the administrative work of state organs, while others, without investigation and study, are content to give vague, generalized direction or direction based on imagination. This is another tendency which must be overcome.

The points I have mentioned about the relationship between the Party and the state organs in their work also generally apply to the relationship between the Party and the various people's organizations. But as democracy in these organizations is much broader than that in state organs, the Party should take this special feature into consideration when exercising leadership over the leading Party members' groups in them.

In order to strengthen unity and solidarity within its own ranks and correctly to play its role as leader and nucleus, the Party has waged uncompromising struggles against all sorts of deviations on this matter. The long-term existence of the Party in widely-scattered rural areas, the strong and persistent influence of feudal, bourgeois and petty-bourgeois ideas and styles of work in our society, and the deepening of class struggle at certain periods of the socialist revolution—all these factors cannot but find reflection in the life of the Party. Therefore, the solidarity and unity of the Party are inseparable from varying degrees of inner-Party struggles.

As we all know, the most serious inner-Party struggle occurring in the interval between the Seventh and Eighth Congresses was the fight against the anti-Party alliance of Gao Gang and Rao Shushi. A detailed report on this struggle was given and discussed at the National Conference of Party Representatives held in March 1955.

The basic characteristic of this anti-Party alliance was its attempt to seize the supreme power of the Party and the state through utterly unprincipled and extensive conspiratorial activities. It tried to maintain exclusive control over certain areas and departments and use them as its "capital" in order to oppose the Central Committee and usurp its authority; with this purpose in view, it carried on agitation against the Central Committee in different areas and in the People's Liberation Army. These conspiratorial activities were diametrically opposed to the interests of the Party and the people, and could only benefit the enemies of the Chinese people. For this reason the National Conference of Party Representatives in March 1955 unanimously endorsed the measures taken in this connection by the Fourth Plenary Session of the Seventh Central Committee held in February 1954 and then by the Political Bureau of the Central Committee.

Since the Fourth Plenary Session of the Seventh Central Committee of the Party and the National Conference of Party Representatives, the Party's solidarity and unity have been immensely strengthened and the political awareness of all Party members and the fighting capacity of the Party organizations have been greatly enhanced. The enemies of the Party and the people gained nothing from this struggle.

The Central Committee decided to expel Gao Gang and Rao Shushi from the Party because their conduct gravely imperilled the interests of the Party and the people and because, over a long period before and after the Fourth Plenary Session of the Seventh Central Committee, they showed no signs of repenting and mending their ways after repeated warnings by the Party. At the National Conference on Financial and Economic Work in the summer of 1953 and, again, at the National Conference on Organizational Work in

September and October of the same year, the Central Committee especially called upon all Party members to strengthen Party solidarity and oppose any acts which might undermine it. But these conspirators, bent on splitting the Party and seizing power, turned a deaf ear to these warnings.

The resolution of the Fourth Plenary Session of the Seventh Central Committee states: "With regard to those who take a stand against the Party, obdurately refuse to correct their errors, or carry on sectarian, schismatic or other harmful activities within the Party", the Party "must conduct relentless struggles and subject them to severe disciplinary measures or even expel them from the Party when necessary; for only by so doing can unity in the Party be safeguarded and the interests of the revolution and the people be defended".

But this is just one side of the Party's policy towards Party members who have made mistakes. The same resolution points out: "Every comrade may have shortcomings and make mistakes, every comrade needs other people's help, and the purpose of Party unity is precisely to develop this kind of comradely mutual help. In dealing with the shortcomings or errors of Party members, we should vary our policy according to different circumstances." The resolution adds: "As for comrades whose shortcomings or errors are relatively unimportant, or those who, though their shortcomings or errors are serious or relatively serious, can still place the interests of the Party above their own and are willing to mend their ways and actually do so after being helped through criticism and education, the principle of curing the sickness to save the patient should be adopted towards them. Serious criticisms must be made of their shortcomings or errors against which the necessary struggles must be waged according to the merit of each case, but not only should such criticism and struggle start out from a position of unity, the aim should also be to reach unity through criticism and struggle. The comrades concerned should not be deprived of the chance to correct their ways. Moreover, their isolated, partial, temporary, relatively unimportant shortcomings or errors should not be deliberately exaggerated into systematic, serious ones; this is not starting out from a position of unity, nor can the aim of unity be attained in this way. Therefore, it is not in the interests of the Party."

The foregoing principles for dealing with the mistakes of Party members, as set forth in the resolution of the Fourth Plenary Session of the Seventh Central Committee, have now been written into the General Programme of the draft Constitution.

As we all know, since 1935 the Central Committee has always acted upon the principle of treating each case on its own merits in dealing with Party members who have made mistakes. Practice has shown that it is correct to adhere to this principle, which is conducive to the unity of the Party and the prosperity of its cause. The Central Committee believes that as a general rule the aim of correcting the mistakes of Party members is to draw lessons, to improve our work and to educate all Party members; in other words, to "learn from past mistakes to avoid future ones", and to "cure the sickness to save the patient". The aim is not to rectify such members "to death"—to make it virtually impossible for them to continue to work in the Party. Therefore, in dealing with such members, we should lay emphasis on a factual analysis of the root cause and essence of their errors, on how to raise their ideological level and on how to draw the correct lesson for other comrades and the whole Party. Stress must not be laid on disciplinary action taken by the Party organization, nor should the problem be solved by the methods of "putting labels" on the offender or by resorting to punishment in a summary way. Unduly severe or indiscriminate punishment is especially to be avoided, for it will create tension and cause fear in the Party, which would be detrimental to the Party's strength. In the period when our Party was dominated by "Left" opportunists, the error was committed of pushing inner-Party struggle to the extreme. A policy of excessively harsh struggle and punishment (what were called "ruthless struggles" and "merciless blows") was pursued within the Party. As a result, Party unity, inner-Party democracy and the initiative of the rank-and-file Party membership all suffered severe damage and the advance of the Party's cause was seriously hindered. Although such wrong treatment of comrades' shortcomings and mistakes is no longer a dominant feature of Party life, it still exists in some organizations, and attention must be paid to rectifying it.

On the other hand, another tendency also deserving of attention exists in the Party. This is to be over-tolerant and over-indulgent towards comrades who have made mistakes without giving them the disciplining they deserve or waging any ideological struggle against them. This is a tendency towards liberalism, which must also be resolutely combated.

In order to maintain Party solidarity and unity on the basis of Marxism–Leninism, to help comrades overcome their shortcomings and rectify mistakes in time, it is necessary to conduct criticism and self-criticism on an extensive scale within the Party. To encourage and support criticism from below and to prohibit the suppression of criticism are of decisive importance for the unfolding of criticism inside the Party. In the past few years, the Central Committee has organized several Party-wide campaigns of criticism and self-criticism in the form of "rectification campaigns" which have yielded remarkably good results. When calling lower-rank comrades to meetings or in talking to them, leading comrades of the Central Committee have taken the initiative in asking them to criticize its work, listened patiently to their criticisms, and promptly taken necessary and practical measures to correct the shortcomings and mistakes pointed out, with the result that inner-Party criticism from below has been greatly encouraged. The Central Committee has engaged in a sharp struggle against the suppression of criticism and applied disciplinary measures to some leading personnel who arbitrarily stifled criticism from below. But it must be admitted that even now not a few responsible comrades in Party organizations and not a few Party members who hold responsible positions in government departments and people's organizations have failed to encourage and support criticism from below. Some of them even use the despicable method of retaliating against their critics. This is another grave sign that the germs of bureaucracy are attacking our Party. Every true Communist must fight to root out this evil.

V

I should now like to make some explanations about the provisions in the draft Constitution regarding Party membership. A number of important changes have been made in the draft as compared with the Constitution adopted at the Seventh Congress. This is because the conditions of the Party and its members now are quite different from what they were at the time of the Seventh Congress. These revisions make higher demands on the members and at the same time extend their rights.

The most significant change about the Party is that it is now in the position of leadership throughout the country. The Party's programme for a democratic revolution has been carried out in nearly all parts of the country, and its programme for a socialist revolution has in the main been successfully carried out. Its present task is to complete the socialist revolution and bring about the socialist industrialization of the country in not too long a period, thus turning China into a mighty socialist industrial country. Organizationally, the composition of the Party has greatly changed both in numerical strength and in the social origin of its members. According to figures provided by the Organization Department of the Central Committee, at the end of June 1956 the Party had a total membership of 10,734,384, which is 1.74 per cent of the total population. Of this, 1,502,814, or 14 per cent of the total membership, are workers; 7,417,459, or 69.1 per cent, are peasants; 1,255,923, or 11.7 per cent, are intellectuals; and 558,188, or 5.2 per cent, are of other social origin. Women constitute about 10 per cent of the total membership.

The triumph of the Party's cause, the increasing weight of its responsibility towards the people, and the rise of its prestige among the masses—all this demands that our Party should set higher standards for its members. Moreover, a person's decision to join our Party generally used to mean that he was prepared to fight for the interests of the masses and for the supreme ideals of human society at the risk of his personal freedom and even of his very life. Nowadays, however, it may easily happen that people join the Party for prestige and position and that, once in the Party, they harm the interests of the masses instead of safeguarding them. To be sure, there are very few such people in our Party, but all the same we cannot neglect this fact. To strive to attain higher standards of Party membership is one of the Party's important political tasks at the present time.

With this end in view, new provisions are made in the draft Constitution regarding the qualifications for Party membership.

In the first place, the draft demands that Party members must be people who work and do not exploit the labour of others. In our day all honour derives solely from labour, and to exploit the labour of others instead of working oneself is a deep disgrace in the eyes of the people. With the progress of socialist transformation, living through the exploitation of other people's labour is dying out in our country. However, in present-day Chinese society there are still exploiters, overt and covert exploitative practices and ideas of the exploiting class. We must not let such people, practices, and ideas find their way into the Party, and we must see to it that every Party member draws a clear line between labour and exploitation.

Concerning the duties of Party members, there is much that is new in the provisions of the draft Constitution as compared with the relevant articles of the existing Constitution.

In the draft it is laid down that one of the duties of Party members is "to safeguard the Party's solidarity and consolidate its unity". The reason for this provision is obvious. Solidarity and unity are the very life of the Party, and it is unthinkable that the Party should have any need for members who do not care for its life.

It is provided in the draft that Party members must energetically fulfil the tasks assigned them by the Party, because this is the concrete guarantee for the implementation of Party policies and decisions.

The draft requires every Party member to strictly observe the Party Constitution and the laws of the state and behave in accordance with communist ethics, no exception being made for any Party member, whatever his contribution or position. Here, the Central Committee considers it of special significance today to stipulate that no Party member, whatever his contribution or position, is allowed to act against the Party Constitution, the laws of the state, or communist ethics. Some Party members who have rendered meritorious service and hold responsible positions do have the idea that they can act as they please, that this is their "prerogative". There are even Party organizations which have given tacit consent to this view. Actually, anyone who entertains or supports it is helping the enemy to corrode our Party. All such people who conduct themselves like "overlords" tend to think that they are indispensable to the Party. But in fact the exact contrary is the case. Not only does our Party have no need of them, it does not permit the presence in its ranks of any "overlords", who in the matter of fulfilling the duties of Party members, act differently from ordinary members. Respect is due a person's contribution and position only if he does not get conceited about them or consider them as something entitling him to "special privileges", and, on the contrary, is even more modest, prudent and conscious of his responsibility to set a good example. Otherwise his conceit and insolence will inevitably be his ruin. The Party will never tolerate such people at the risk of isolating itself from the broad masses.

The draft stipulates that it is the duty of every Party member to practise criticism and self-criticism, expose shortcomings and mistakes in work and strive to overcome and correct them and that it is his duty to report such shortcomings and mistakes to the leading Party bodies, up to and including the Central Committee. Without doubt this provision in the draft will serve to arouse the political enthusiasm of all Party members, promote inner-Party criticism and facilitate the exposure and elimination of shortcomings and mistakes in Party work.

The draft provides that Party members should be truthful and honest with the Party and not conceal or distort the truth. This is a principle of vital significance in Party life. To proceed from reality and seek truth from facts is our fundamental viewpoint as materialists. Any concealment of the facts from the Party or their distortion can only do harm to the Party. And in the end, too, it can bring only harm to the very people who conceal or distort facts.

The draft also requires Party members to be constantly on the alert against the intrigues of the enemy and to safeguard the classified information of the Party and the state.

All these new provisions concerning the duties of Party members indicate that the Party is making stricter demands than before on its members.

It is necessary to conduct a broad and deep-going education in the duties of Party members among the membership and among activists who want to join the Party. When a Party member fails to fulfil his duties, the Party organization should promptly criticize and educate him. Many Party members, especially new ones, have failed in their duties because they do not really know what their duties are, or because they do not understand the real meaning of the relevant articles in the Party Constitution, although they have read them. Therefore, timely criticism and education are often sufficient to help a Party member avoid making similar or bigger mistakes in future, when he fails in his duties for the first time. In such cases, it is wrong to rashly take disciplinary measures.

Education by itself, however, will not ensure that all Party members strictly observe their duties. The draft Party Constitution provides that any serious infraction of these duties, sabotage of Party unity, infringement of the laws of the state, violation of Party decisions, damage to Party interests, or deception towards the Party, constitutes a violation of Party discipline, and disciplinary action shall be taken against it.

Applicants for Party membership must go through the procedure for admission individually. The draft Constitution stipulates that an applicant must be recommended by two Party members of full standing and is admitted as a probationary member after being accepted by the general membership meeting of the Party branch and being approved by the next higher Party committee, and he may become a Party member of full standing only after the completion of a probationary period of one year.

In the draft, the term "probationary period" has been adopted in place of "candidature", which has long been in use, and the term "probationary member" in place of "candidate member". This is because the term probationary is more accurate in meaning. The change was suggested by someone outside the Party and we have accepted the suggestion.

During the discussion of the draft, many comrades raised the question: "If it is our purpose to raise the standards of Party membership, why have we discarded the original provisions about different procedures of admission for applicants of different social origin? Might this not affect the purity of the Party?"

The distinction previously made in the procedure of admitting new members has been removed because the former classification of social origin has lost or is losing its original meaning. Both before the Seventh Congress and for a considerable period after it was essential to have different procedures of admission for applicants of different social origin, and this served a very good purpose. But in recent years the situation has drastically changed. The difference between workers and office employees is now only a matter of a division of labour within the same class. Casual labourers and farm labourers have disappeared. Poor and middle peasants have all become members of agricultural producers' co-operatives, and before long the distinction between them will become merely a thing of historical interest. With the introduction of the conscription system, revolutionary soldiers no longer constitute an independent social stratum. The vast majority of our intellectuals have now come over politically to the side of the working class, and a rapid change is taking place in their family background. The conditions in which the urban poor and the professional people used to exist as independent social strata are virtually no longer present. Every year, large numbers of peasants and students become workers, large numbers of workers, peasants and their sons and daughters join the ranks of the intellectuals and office-workers, large numbers of peasants, students, workers and office-workers join the army and become revolutionary soldiers, while large numbers of revolutionary soldiers return to civilian life as peasants, students, workers or office-workers. What is the point, then, of classifying these social strata into two different categories? And even if we were to try and devise a classification, how could we make it neat and clear-cut?

It has already been stated that only those who work and do not exploit the labour of others and only those who are qualified for Party membership can be admitted to the Party. Therefore, the procedural problem has ceased to exist with regard to people of different social origin.

Practice has proved that the main problems in purifying the ranks of the Party lie in: strengthening supervision over the work of recruiting new members, seeing to it that the general membership meeting of the Party branch and the Party committee of the next higher level check up carefully on applicants and on probationary members at the end of their probationary period, carefully observing probationary members and giving them education during their probationary period, giving timely education to Party members who are not fully up to the standard, and expelling whatever bad elements have wormed their way into the Party. Purity does not depend on the number of Party members required for recommending different types of applicants, the length of Party standing of such members or the length of the probationary period for probationary members.

The present membership of our Party is nine times what it was at the time of the Seventh Congress. How were the new members admitted into the Party? Are they really qualified for Party membership? Judging from the results of past Party rectification campaigns, the overwhelming majority of them were admitted according to the procedures laid down in the Party Constitution and were qualified for Party membership. On the whole, the Party organizations have grown up in the course of mass revolutionary struggles, and the very fact that those who were admitted were people active among the masses and tested in struggle forms the chief guarantee for the quality of the Party membership. But mistakes were made on many occasions in the matter of admitting new members. During the War of Liberation, new members were recruited in the rural districts of some liberated areas through launching "Campaigns to Join the Party" or through a process of "self-nomination, public discussion, and approval by the Party organization". In the two years just before and after the liberation of the whole country, the membership of the Party grew with undue speed, and in some areas it grew practically without guidance and without plan, while in others Party organizations even went about recruiting new members in large numbers and setting up Party branches before the masses were aroused. The result was that certain Party organizations were at one point impure to a high degree. On the other hand, the mistake of "closed-door" sectarianism was also made in admitting new members. For instance, at one time the Party failed to attach importance to recruiting new members from among industrial workers, at another it neglected to recruit new members from among revolutionary intellectuals, and in certain rural areas the Party organizations neglected to recruit activists among youth and women.

In any case, it is an obvious fact that roughly 90 per cent of the present 10,730,000 members have joined our Party since the Seventh Congress. Experience has shown time and again that many members, although they have joined the Party organizationally, have not yet joined it ideologically or at least not wholly joined ideologically. It is, therefore, the task of the Party organizations at all levels to make a conscientious effort and conduct more effective education among the vast numbers of new members, to take practical measures to organize and guide their study of Marxism–Leninism, Comrade Mao Zedong's writings and the history and policy of our Party and to strengthen their education in proletarian internationalism, so as to raise their level of political awareness and enable them to become genuinely qualified ideologically as Party members.

The ranks of the Party have expanded rapidly. But the number of Party members is still very small among certain sections of the people, in certain enterprises, offices and educational institutions, in certain villages and among certain nationalities. At the same time, more and more activists are coming to the fore and asking to join our fighting ranks. Therefore, apart from striving to improve the quality of the membership, the Party must continue in a planned way to admit those who apply for membership and are fully qualified for it. The Party should specially strengthen its work among women and pay attention to recruiting those who are advanced.

While striving to raise the standards of its members, the Party must pay attention to the protection and extension of their democratic rights. The draft Constitution contains some new and important provisions regarding the rights of members.

It is laid down in the draft that Party members enjoy the right of giving full play to their creative ability in work. This is of significance as a principle. It will greatly stimulate vast numbers of Party members to endeavour, so far as is compatible with Party discipline, to concentrate the wisdom of the masses, to think independently and to solve problems practically and creatively. Moreover, it will enable those leading personnel who are stuck in a rut and never set store by the creative ability of rank-and-file Party members to learn and change their style of work, and this, too, will help inner-Party democracy to flourish.

The draft provides that Party members enjoy the right to ask to attend in person when a Party organization decides to take disciplinary action against them or make an appraisal of their strong and weak points. This means that the Party organization will have the opportunity to listen to the member's own statement so that no decision will be made on the basis of inaccurate or one-sided reports. This procedure has already been generally adopted in the Party, but there are certain Party organizations which have not put it into effect. Without any reason whatsoever, they often fail to let the members know until they have decided on the disciplinary measures to be taken against them. Of course, there are special cases in which it is impossible for the Party member concerned to attend in person when such a decision is made by a Party organization. But such cases should be regarded as the exception rather than the rule. And even in such cases, the member concerned still has the right to ask beforehand to attend in person and the right to appeal afterwards if he disagrees with the decision made by the Party organization.

The draft Party Constitution provides that Party members enjoy the right to reserve their opinions or submit them to a leading body of the Party if they disagree with any Party decision, although, in the meantime, they must unconditionally carry out such decisions. We all know that the Party is an organization based on ideological unity and that the ideological unity of the membership is the foundation of the solidarity and unity of the Party. But this does not mean that no Party member should hold any opinions different from Party decisions. No, this is impossible. The unity that the Party demands is an ideological unity on all questions concerning the Party's basic principles and unity of action on all practical issues. In matters of day-to-day work, not only is it permissible for some differing views to exist among Party members, but it is unavoidable. In order to get various practical problems solved, the Party must act according to the principle that the individual is subordinate to the organization, the minority is subordinate to the majority, the lower level is subordinate to the higher level, and all Party organizations are subordinate to the Central Committee. In this connection, it is entirely correct and necessary for the Party to demand that members who hold different views must unconditionally carry out Party decisions in their actions. Even so, the Party members concerned still have the right to reserve their own opinions and to submit them to the Party organizations to which they belong and to higher bodies, while the Party organizations should not compel them to give up their opinions by means of disciplinary action. Far from harming the Party, these provisions can have a good effect. Provided that the Party's decisions are correct and the Party members who hold different views are willing to bow before the truth, these members will eventually be glad to acknowledge the correctness of the Party and admit their own mistakes. If, on the other hand, truth eventually turns out to be on the side of the minority, then the protection of the right of the minority will help the Party to recognize the truth.

In comparison with the corresponding articles in the existing Constitution, the draft makes fuller provisions with regard to the right of members to participate in free and practical discussion at Party meetings or in the Party press on theoretical and practical questions relating to Party policy; their right to criticize any Party organization or any functionary at Party meetings; and their right to address any statement, appeal or complaint to any Party organization, up to and including the Central Committee.

The draft stipulates that infringement of the rights of Party members constitutes a violation of Party discipline and disciplinary action shall be taken against it. This provides an effective guarantee of the rights of Party members.

With regard to commendation and disciplinary measures in the Party, the draft Constitution contains the following important changes: first, the old provisions regarding commendation have been taken out; secondly, the provisions concerning disciplinary measures applicable to entire Party organizations have also been taken out; and thirdly, the provisions concerning disciplinary measures applicable to Party members have been simplified.

Everyday reality has proved that it is not appropriate to make "admonition" a disciplinary measure and that many inconveniences arise from dividing warning into two kinds, private and public. As for disciplinary measures against entire Party organizations it is wholly feasible to replace them with disciplinary measures against individual members.

Some comrades ask: "Why must the provisions for commendation be taken out?" It too is what the realities of everyday life have taught us. Although provisions regarding commendation were made in the Party Constitution adopted by the Seventh Congress, the experience of the last eleven years has proved them to be unnecessary. Of course this does not mean that the Party takes no notice of the excellent work done by many of its finest members; it has publicized their achievements and experience and promoted them to important posts according to their personal qualities and abilities. All this is the Party's commendation of these members. But there is a more important reason for removing these provisions. Fundamentally speaking, we Communists do not work for the sake of being commended. We work for the good of the people. When we have worked energetically and correctly and have consequently won the confidence of the people, this is the highest reward possible for Communist Party members.

Here I feel it necessary to speak about the question of Party cadres. Truly, if we make strict demands on every rank-and-file Party member, we need to make still stricter ones on Party cadres. Even more than rank-and-file members they enjoy the confidence of the Party and the people and consequently shoulder a greater responsibility to them. According to rough and ready statistics, there are altogether over 300,000 Party cadres at or above the rank of county Party committee members. The quality of the work of these 300,000-odd people has a decisive bearing on the cause of the Party. These cadres ought to be the first in learning never to become separated from the masses, never to feel self-complacent, never to be afraid of difficulties, and always to be ready to accept criticism from below, to improve their work and to patiently educate those who are working under their leadership through their personal example.

It would be superfluous to explain the fact that since the Seventh Congress, and especially since 1949, there has been a great increase in the number of Party cadres. Nevertheless, there remains a universal feeling that there are not enough of them. This shows that there are still serious defects in the selection and promotion of cadres. The chief of these is that even today many comrades still use "seniority" as the criterion in selecting cadres. Party members of long standing with a rich store of experience are undoubtedly a valuable asset to the Party. But we should be making a very grievous mistake if we value this asset to the exclusion of everything else, because our revolutionary cause is advancing and the number of cadres required is increasing all the time, while the number of old Party members is necessarily falling. This being so, if we don't resolutely and confidently employ carefully-selected new cadres, what other outcome can there be except harm to the cause of the Party and the people?

In order to keep up with the rapid development of our cause, one important task of the Party is to train and promote large numbers of new cadres and help them to familiarize themselves with their work and establish a comradely relationship with the older cadres, a relationship of unity and solidarity and of learning from one another. The Party must pay particular attention to the training of cadres to master production techniques or other branches of professional knowledge, because cadres with such qualifications are the basic force for the building of socialism. In all localities our Party must train native cadres who are familiar with local conditions and have close ties with the local people. In areas inhabited by minority nationalities the Party must do its utmost to train local minority nationality cadres. Our Party must be very firmly resolved to train and promote women cadres and help and encourage them to advance unceasingly, since women form one of the greatest reservoirs of Party cadres.

In our work regarding the management of cadres, an important improvement in the last few years has been the division of management according to rank and department so that it can be co-ordinated with political and professional inspection and supervision. The Party should strive to improve its management of cadres further in this direction, so that cadres at all posts and in all departments will be under the careful supervision of the Party and receive its concrete help, and the quality of cadres themselves will thus be constantly raised. This is also an essential prerequisite for steadily raising the quality of all rank-and-file Party members.

VI

With regard to the organizational structure of the Party, besides giving the Party congresses from county level upwards a fixed term of office and abolishing the conferences of Party representatives at all levels provided for in the existing Constitution, the draft Party Constitution contains a number of other new provisions, namely, those concerning the central, local and primary organizations, control organs, and the Party's relationship with the Communist Youth League. In this connection, only a few brief explanations are needed.

In the section dealing with the central organizations, the draft provides that the Central Committee, which elects the Political Bureau, shall also elect the Standing Committee of the Political Bureau, which will take over the role formerly fulfilled by the Secretariat, a role proved both expedient and necessary by the long experience of our Party. The Central Committee will also elect the Secretariat, which in future will attend to the Central Committee's day-to-day work under the direction of the Political Bureau and its Standing Committee. Owing to the pressure of Party and government work, the existing central organs are already proving inadequate. Hence the Central Committee finds it essential to set up additional central organs. It also finds it necessary to have a number of vice-chairmen and a general secretary; the chairman and vice-chairmen of the Central Committee will concurrently be the chairman and vice-chairmen of the Political Bureau.

In the section dealing with local Party organizations, the draft sets forth the system for the Party organizations of the provinces, autonomous regions, municipalities directly under the central authority, autonomous prefectures, counties, autonomous counties and other municipalities. In view of the increasingly complicated nature of the work of the leading bodies of the local Party organizations, the draft provides that a standing committee and a secretariat shall be set up under the Party committee of each of these organizations. In order to reduce the number of organizational levels, the draft provides that, within the limits of their respective regions, prefectural committees shall act as the representative bodies of provincial or autonomous region committees, and the district committees shall likewise act as the representative bodies of the Party committees for municipalities directly under the central authority or of the municipal, county or autonomous county committees. As a matter of fact, in certain provinces some of the prefectural committees and district committees in rural areas have already been abolished.

As the membership of the primary Party organizations ranges from a minimum of three up to ten thousand, it is necessary to allow the greatest flexibility in their organizational form. The draft divides the primary Party organizations into three categories. The first comprises primary organizations with a hundred or more Party members, which may set up primary Party committees, each with a number of branches or general branches under them. The second comprises primary organizations with fifty to ninety-nine members, which may set up general branch committees, each with a number of branches under them. The third category comprises primary organizations with less than fifty members, which may set up branch committees. The draft also contains certain other provisions conducive to flexibility. In the course of implementation it is possible that there will be units for which none of the three foregoing forms will be found entirely suitable, in which case the competent Party committees can regard them as special cases and deal with them flexibly as they see fit.

As for the tasks of the primary organizations, fairly comprehensive provisions are made to suit present conditions. The draft stipulates that in enterprises, villages, schools and army units primary Party organizations must guide and supervise the work of the administrative bodies and mass organizations in their units. It points out that in public institutions and organizations they should watch over the ideology of all Party members working in these units and that they should report any shortcomings in their work without delay to the administrative heads of these units and to higher Party organizations. At present, many primary Party organizations are not carrying out these tasks.

Inasmuch as primary organizations form the basic links between the Party and the broad masses, it is an important political task of the Party's leading bodies to constantly check up on and help improve their work. But in both urban and rural areas there are leading bodies which are prone to busy themselves assigning one task after another to the primary organizations, but seldom check up on how they are conducting their work or give any concrete help, ideological or otherwise, to their members. In

PLATE 1. Deng Xiaoping with Chairman Mao Zedong.

PLATE 2. Deng Xiaoping with Chairman Mao Zedong, Liu Shaoqi, Zhu De, Zhou Enlai and Chen Yun.

PLATE 3. Deng Xiaoping in Yanan in 1938. *From right*: Xu Haidong, He Long, Peng Dehuai, Zhou Enlai, Zhu De, Deng Xiaoping, Teng Daiyuan, Luo Ronghuan, Xiao Ke, Guan Xiangying, Cheng Zihua.

PLATE 4. Liu Bocheng and Deng Xiaoping personally direct the preparations for crossing the Chang Jiang River (Yangtze River) prior to the crossing of the river by a million valiant PLA soldiers.

PLATE 5. Deng Xiaoping at the Headquarters of the 2nd Field Army of the People's Liberation Army in 1949 when the PLA were marching on' to Southwest China.

PLATE 6. Deng Xiaoping on an inspection tour in Kunming on 25 October 1958.

PLATE 7. Zhu De and Deng Xiaoping viewing high yield sorghum in Dongfanghong (East is Red) Commune, Luwangzhuang township, Funing County, Hebei Province in August 1958.

PLATE 8. Deng Xiaoping with Chen Yi, Peng Zhen, Yang Shangkun and Li Fuchun in Beijing in the spring of 1963.

PLATE 9. Deng Xiaoping greeting Premier Zhou Enlai and Vice-Premier Chen Yi back home from Cairo in July 1965.

PLATE 10. Meeting with General Secretary Nicolae Ceausescu of the Romanian Communist Party on 16 April 1982.

PLATE 11. Deng Xiaoping with Zhao Ziyang and Wu Kehua in Chengdu in February 1978.

PLATE 12. Deng Xiaoping having a cordial conversation with Kim Il Sung on 8 September 1978.

PLATE 13. Deng Xiaoping accepting the title of honorary LL.D from the Temple University on 31 January 1979 in Blair House, Washington D.C.

PLATE 14. Deng Xiaoping helping with the planting of trees on 12 February 1979.

PLATE 15. Deng Xiaoping and Li Xiannian viewing murals and other paintings in the lounge of the Capital Airport in October 1979.

PLATE 16. Cordially chatting with Mme Soong Ching Ling and Mme Luo Shuzhang at a tea party hosted by the Chinese People's Political Consultative Conference on New Year's Day 1980.

PLATE 17. Deng Xiaoping at a plenary session of the Eleventh Central Committee of the Communist Party of China in February 1980.

PLATE 18. Deng Xiaoping interviewed by a Luxemburg TV correspondent on 19 April 1980.

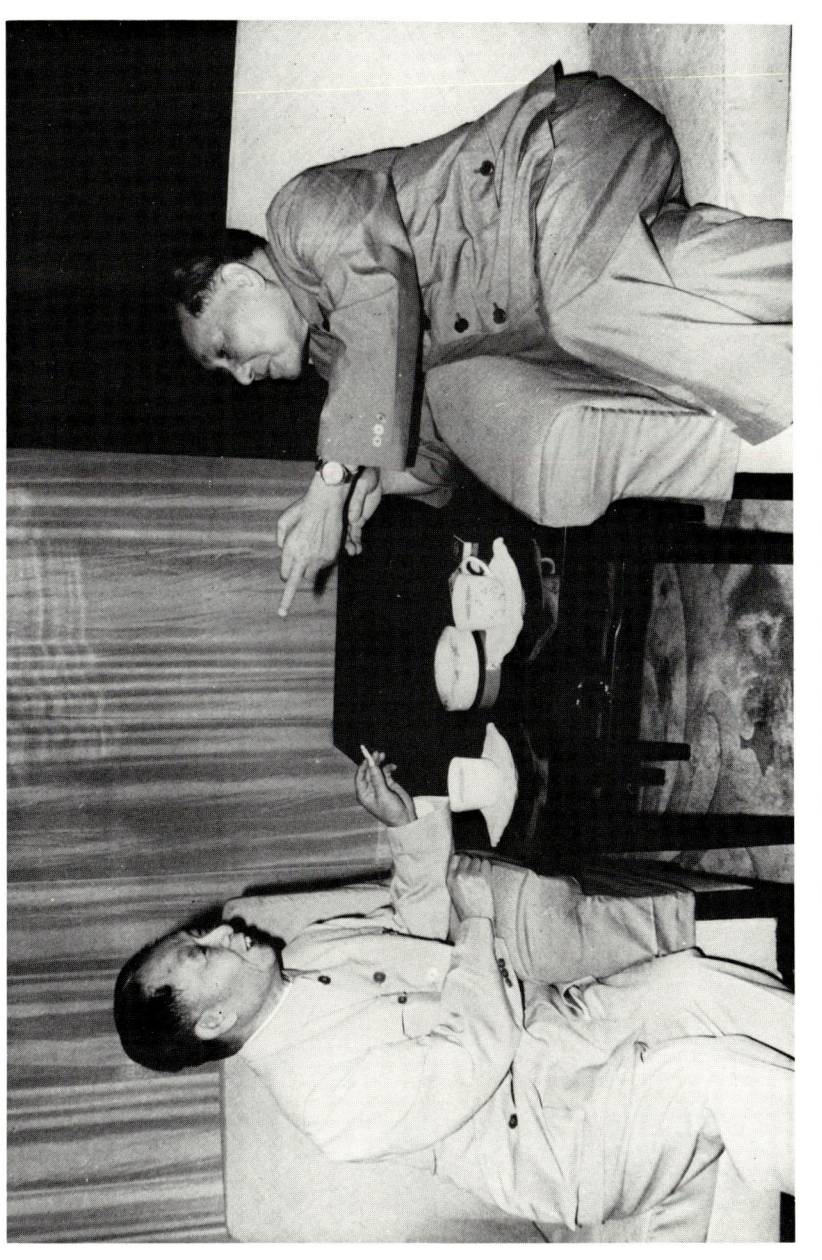
PLATE 19. With Hu Yaobang in September 1980.

PLATE 20. Deng Xiaoping delivering a speech during a military parade in 1981.

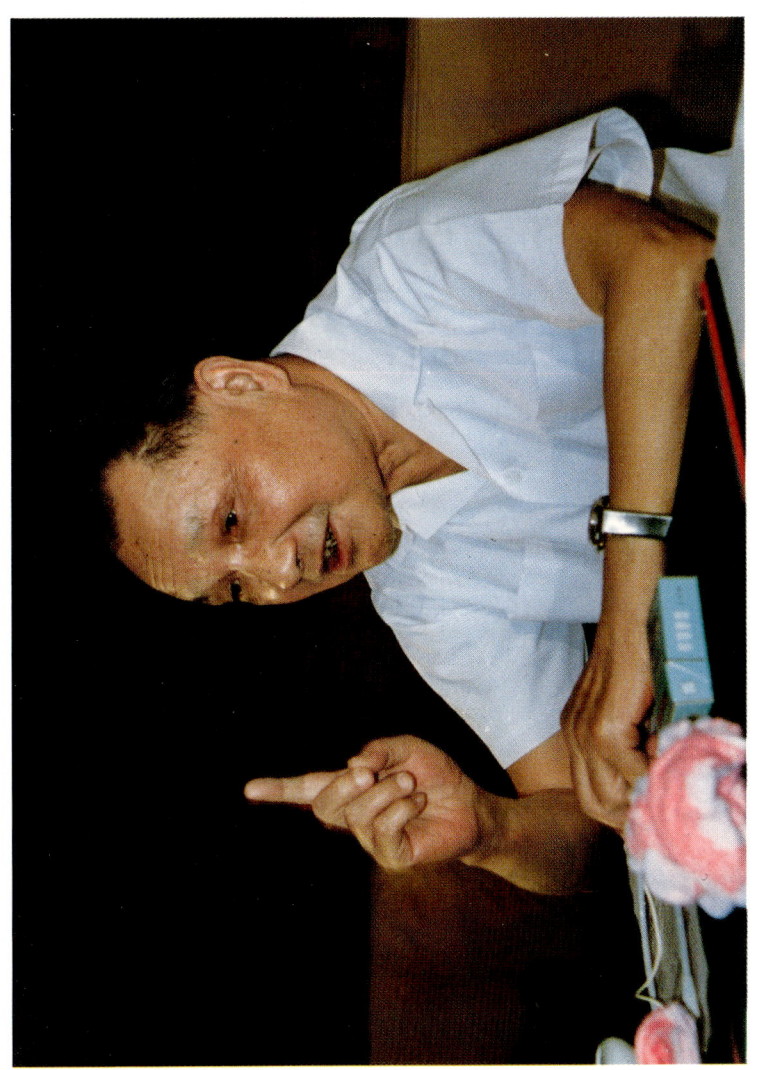

PLATE 21. Deng Xiaoping at a closing plenary session of the Eleventh Central Committee of the Communist Party of China on 29 June 1981.

PLATE 22. Deng Xiaoping in Urumqi in August 1981.

PLATE 23. Deng Xiaoping enjoying a performance of national songs and dances in Urumqi.

Plate 24. Deng Xiaoping in the midst of people visiting the Yinian Hall in Zhongnanhai, Beijing, on 17 April 1983.

PLATE 25. Deng Xiaoping inspecting the Tianchi meteorological station on Changbai Mountains in the natural protection zone of Changbai Mountains, Jilin Province, on 13 August 1983.

Plate 26. Deng Xiaoping inspecting the Xiamen Special Economic Region in February 1984.

PLATE 27. Deng Xiaoping inspecting the Shenzhen Special Economic Region on 25 January 1984.

PLATE 28. Deng Xiaoping with Hu Yaobang, Zhao Ziyang, Li Xiannian and Norodom Sihanouk on the Rostrum of the Tiananmen Gate on 1 October 1984.

Plate 29. Deng Xiaoping reviewing the Military Parade on National Day, 1 October 1984.

accordance with the Constitution, all Party committees that are directly responsible for leading primary organizations should conduct extensive education among them and at the same time draw conclusions necessary for improving their leadership over these organizations.

To set up the control organs of the Party at different levels on a sound basis is of great importance to the struggle against unhealthy tendencies within the Party. Although it was only after the National Conference of Party Representatives held in March 1955 that the Central Control Commission and the control commissions at lower levels began to be set up on the basis of the former discipline inspection commissions, the work of these control commissions has already proved effective. The draft defines the tasks of the control organs and the relationship between higher and lower control commissions. The commissions should not confine themselves to dealing with individual cases as they arise, but should work actively to find out how the Party Constitution, Party discipline, communist ethics and state laws and decrees are being observed by Party members. To this end, the Party committees at different levels must ensure that the control commissions are adequately staffed and must give them constant and vigorous support.

The whole history of the Communist Youth League shows that the League is the Party's reliable reserve force as well as its capable assistant. When the League organization was restored in 1949, it was known by the name of the China New-Democratic Youth League. Since then the membership of the League has grown to 20,000,000, and its energetic activities can be seen on all fronts. In view of the progress of socialist transformation in China and the spread of communist education among our youth, the Central Committee of the Youth League has decided to suggest to the forthcoming national congress of the League that it be renamed the Communist Youth League of China. The Central Committee of the Party believes that this decision is correct. The draft Constitution sets forth the relationship between the Party and the Youth League. It requires Party organizations at all levels to show deep concern for the League's ideological and organizational work, to give guidance to the League in imbuing all its members with the communist spirit and educating them in Marxist–Leninist theory, to see to it that close contact is maintained between the League and the large numbers of young people and to pay constant attention to selecting members for the leading core of the League. The youth represent our future: it is they who will carry on all our undertakings. Therefore, we are convinced that Party organizations at all levels will spare no effort or energy in carrying out these tasks.

★ ★ ★ ★ ★

In the foregoing, I have made some necessary explanations of the draft Party Constitution put forward by the Central Committee. The Committee holds that this draft is adapted to our Party's present conditions and tasks.

The Central Committee believes that this Constitution, after being discussed and adopted by the Eighth National Party Congress, will become a powerful instrument by means of which we shall further raise the quality of the Party, broaden the scope of inner-Party democracy, bring into full play the political initiative of the Party membership, improve the Party's organizational work, and strengthen its solidarity and unity and its fighting capacity.

As I have already said, the draft Party Constitution does not differ in fundamental principle from the Constitution adopted by the Seventh Congress. And it must be added that the fundamental spirit of the draft Constitution is nothing but a logical development of the various principles laid down by the Seventh Congress to govern the Party's work. Thoroughgoing discussion was conducted and correct decisions were made at the Seventh Congress on such issues as the Party's mass line, democratic centralism, the solidarity and unity of the Party, the raising of the standards of Party membership and protection of members' rights. Thanks to this, since the Seventh Congress, our Party has been full of vigour in its organizational work and has become steadily more flourishing in the same way that it has flourished in its political struggles. The Party's organizational work has ensured the successful fulfilment of its political tasks. In the eleven years between the Seventh and Eighth Congresses, our Party's organizational strength has grown rapidly, its ties with the masses have been greatly extended and strengthened, inner-Party life has become increasingly active, the Party's ranks have become more closely united than at any period in the past, and consequently the achievements won in the Party's cause have also been greater than at any period in the past.

We have made mistakes and met with dangers in our work, and there are still shortcomings and difficulties to be overcome, but none of these has caused, or ever will cause, panic in our Party. On the contrary, our Party always has boundless confidence in itself and the courage to correct mistakes, overcome dangers, remove shortcomings and surmount difficulties, and so strive for fresh and greater victories.

Our Party owes its victories, first and foremost, to the people's trust and support and to the arduous struggles put up by the entire Party membership. We must forever be grateful to and cherish the memory of the martyrs who laid down their lives for the cause of the Party.

Our Party also owes its victories to the leading personnel of the Party organizations at all levels, and particularly to the leader of our Party, Comrade Mao Zedong.

Now our Party is confronted with new and arduous tasks. We must carry through the great task of socialist transformation, fulfil ahead of schedule and overfulfil the First Five-Year Plan for the development of our national economy, and actively prepare to carry out the Second Five-Year Plan, so as to bring about a great advance in our industry, agriculture, communications, transport and commerce, promote our scientific and cultural work, and raise the people's standard of living to a new level. We must liberate Taiwan. We must actively contribute our efforts towards the safeguarding of world peace. To be ready for such great tasks, we must do our utmost to further consolidate our Party and cement the ties between it and the masses of the people.

The Communist Party of China, which is built and has grown on Marxist–Leninist principles and which, through practice, has ceaselessly improved its organization and work and strengthened its ties with the masses, will, with its solidarity and unity, certainly be able to accomplish the glorious tasks the people have entrusted to it.

Speech at the Opening Ceremony of the National Conference on Science

18 March 1978

Comrades,

The successful convocation of this National Conference on Science is a source of great joy for us and for people throughout the country. The very fact that today we are holding this grand gathering, unparalleled in the history of science in China, clearly indicates that the days are gone forever when the Gang of Four—Wang Hongwen, Zhang Chunqiao, Jiang Qing and Yao Wenyuan—could wantonly sabotage the cause of science and persecute intellectuals. Never before have the whole Party and people been so interested in science and technology and given them so much attention. Vast numbers of scientists, technicians, workers, peasants and armymen are actively participating in the movement for scientific experiment. Young people are becoming interested in science and eager to study it. The entire nation is setting out with tremendous enthusiasm on the march towards the modernization of our science and technology. Splendid prospects lie before us.

Among those attending this conference there are outstanding scientists and technicians in various fields, highly able technical innovators, model labourers in scientific farming, and cadres devoted to the Party's tasks in the scientific field. You have all worked diligently for the progress of science and technology in our socialist motherland and made outstanding contributions in this regard. On behalf of the Central Committee of the Communist Party of China, I thank you and salute you.

Comrades,

Our people are undertaking the historic mission of modernizing our agriculture, industry, national defence and science and technology within the present century, in order to transform China into a modern and powerful socialist state. We have waged a bitter struggle against the Gang of

Four over the question of whether the four modernizations are needed or not. The Gang made the senseless statement that "the day the four modernizations programme is realized will mark the day of capitalist restoration". Their sabotage brought China's economy to the brink of collapse and led to a constant widening of the gap between us and the countries with the most advanced science and technology. Did the Gang really want to build socialism and oppose the restoration of capitalism? Not in the least. On the contrary, socialism sustained grave damage wherever their influence was strongest. Their misdeeds, serving as a negative example, make us realize all the more clearly that even though we have a dictatorship of the proletariat, unless we modernize our country, raise our scientific and technological level, develop our productive forces and thus strengthen our country and improve the material and cultural life of our people—unless we do all this, our socialist political and economic system cannot be fully consolidated, and there can be no sure guarantee for the country's security. The more our agriculture, industry, national defence and science and technology are modernized, the stronger we will be in the struggle against forces which sabotage socialism, and the more our people will support the socialist system. Only if we make our country a modern, powerful, socialist state can we more effectively consolidate the socialist system and cope with foreign aggression and subversion; only then can we be reasonably certain of gradually creating the material conditions for the advance to our great goal of communism.

The key to the four modernizations is the modernization of science and technology. Without modern science and technology, it is impossible to build modern agriculture, modern industry or modern national defence. Without the rapid development of science and technology, there can be no rapid development of the economy. The Central Committee of the Party decided to call this national science conference in order to bring home to the Party and country the importance of science, to map out a programme, to commend advanced units and individuals and to discuss measures for speeding up the development of science and technology in China. Today, I would like to speak on some pertinent points.

The first point is the necessity of understanding that science and technology are part of the productive forces. The Gang of Four raised a hue and cry over this, confounding right and wrong and sowing much confusion in people's minds. Marxism has consistently treated science and technology as part of the productive forces. More than a century ago, Marx said that expansion of the use of machinery in production requires the conscious application of natural science. Science too, he said, is among the productive forces. The development of modern science and technology has bound science and production ever more tightly together. It is becoming increasingly clear that science and technology are of tremendous significance as productive forces.

Modern science and technology are now undergoing a great revolution. The advances over the last three decades have not been limited to particular scientific theories or production techniques, nor have they just represented progress and reform in the usual sense. Rather, profound changes have taken place and new leaps have been made in almost all areas. A whole range of new sciences and technologies is continuously emerging. Modern science opens the way for the improvement of production techniques and determines the direction of their development. Many new instruments of production and technical processes first come into being in the laboratory. A series of new industries, including high-polymer synthesis, atomic energy, electronic computers, semi-conductors, astronautics and lasers, have been founded on the basis of newly emerging sciences. Of course both now and in the future there will be many topics of theoretical research for which at the moment no practical application can be seen. But a host of historical facts have proved that once a major breakthrough is achieved in theoretical research, it leads, sooner or later, to enormous progress in production and technology. Contemporary natural science is being applied to production on an unprecedented scale and with unprecedented speed. This has given all fields of material production an entirely new look. In particular, the development of electronic computers, cybernetics and automation technology is rapidly raising the degree of automation in production. With the same manpower and the same number of man-hours, people can turn out scores or hundreds of times more products than before. What has brought about the tremendous advances in the productive forces and the vast increase in labour productivity? Mainly the power of science, the power of technology.

We all know that the basic factors in the productive forces are the means of production and labour power. What is the relationship of science and technology to these two factors? Throughout history, the means of production have always been linked with a given type of science and technology, and, likewise, labour power has always meant labour power armed with a certain degree of knowledge of science and technology. We often say that man is the most active productive force. "Man" here refers to people who possess a certain amount of scientific knowledge, experience in production and skill in the use of tools to create material wealth. There were vast differences between the instruments of production man used, his mastery of scientific knowledge, and his production experience and skills in the Stone, Bronze and Iron Ages and in the seventeenth, eighteenth and nineteenth centuries. Today, the rapid progress of science and technology is speeding up the introduction of new production equipment and new technological processes. Many products are superseded in a matter of a few years by a new generation of products. Only by acquiring a higher level of scientific and general knowlege, richer experience in production and more advanced skills can the worker expand his role in modern production. In our society, the workers have a high degree of political awareness and study assiduously for the conscious purpose of raising their level of scientific and general knowledge, so they will doubtless be able to achieve a higher productivity of labour than that under capitalism.

The recognition that science and technology are productive forces leads in turn to the following question: How should the mental labour involved in scientific research be regarded? Now that science and technology are becoming increasingly important productive forces, should scientists and technicians be considered as workers or not?

In societies under the rule of exploiting classes, there are various kinds of mental workers. Some are wholly in the service of the reactionary ruling classes and thus stand in an antagonistic relationship to manual workers. But even in such a situation, as Lenin said, many of the intellectuals engaged in scientific and technical work are themselves not capitalists but scholars, even though they are filled with bourgeois prejudices. The fruits of their work are used by the exploiters, but in general this is determined by the social system and not by their own free choice. They are totally different from those politicians who rack their brains for expedients of direct service to the reactionary ruling classes. Marx pointed out that ordinary engineers and technicians join in the creation of surplus value. That is to say, they, too, are exploited by the capitalists.

In a socialist society, the mental workers trained by the working class itself are different from intellectuals in any exploitative society past or present. Comrade Mao Zedong pointed out during the period of socialist transformation in China that intellectuals from the old society became faced with the question of which "skin" to attach themselves to. Class contradictions and class struggle continue to exist throughout the historical period of socialism, and so throughout this period, intellectuals must decide whether or not they will adopt and maintain the stand of the working class. But generally speaking, the overwhelming majority of them are already intellectuals serving the working class and other working people. It can therefore be said that they are already part of the working class itself. They differ from the manual workers only insofar as they perform different roles in the social division of labour. Everyone who works, whether with his hands or with his brain, is part of the working people in a socialist society. With the advance of modern science and technology and with progress in the four modernizations, a great deal of heavy manual work will gradually be taken over by machines. Among workers directly engaged in production, manual labour will steadily decrease while mental labour will constantly increase. Moreover, there will be a growing demand for researchers and for scientists and technicians. The Gang of Four distorted the division of labour between mental and manual work in our society today, misrepresenting it as a class antagonism. Their aim was to attack and persecute intellectuals, undermine the alliance between the workers and peasants and the intellectuals, damage the productive forces, and sabotage our socialist revolution and construction.

Science and technology are part of the productive forces. Mental workers who serve socialism are part of the working people. A correct understanding of these two facts is essential to the rapid development of our scientific enterprises. Once we have accepted these premises, it follows that we must make every effort to develop scientific research and education in science and to encourage the revolutionary initiative of our scientific, technical and educational workers. For this is essential if we are to accomplish the four modernizations in the short space of twenty-odd years and bring about a gigantic growth in our productive forces.

Our science and technology have made enormous progress since the founding of New China and have played a vital role in economic construction and in building up our national defence. All this would have been unthinkable in the old China. No one can deny this impressive achievement. But we must be clear-sighted and recognize that there is still an enormous gap between the level of our science and technology and that of the most advanced countries, and that our scientific and technical forces are still too meagre to meet the needs of our modernization programme. In particular, we have lost a lot of time as a result of the sabotage by Lin Biao and the Gang of Four.

Where do we stand in terms of production technology? Several hundred million people are occupied in producing food, and the problem of grain has not really been solved yet. Labour productivity in our iron and steel industry is only a small percentage of that achieved in the advanced countries. The gap is still wider in the newer industries. In the latter, a lag of only three to five years—to say nothing of eight to ten or ten to twenty—creates a really big gap.

Comrade Mao Zedong often reminded us that China ought to make a greater contribution to humanity. In ancient times, China scored brilliant achievements in science and technology; its four great inventions (paper, printing, the compass and gunpowder) played a major role in advancing world civilization. We should not rest on our ancestors' achievements; rather such achievements should strengthen our resolve to catch up with and surpass the countries that are most advanced in science and technology. Our present contributions in these fields are far from commensurate with the standing of a socialist country such as ours.

Will people be discouraged if we point out this backwardness as an objective fact? Some people, perhaps. But such people don't know the first thing about Marxism. As for us proletarian revolutionaries, stating the facts and making a serious analysis of their historical and current causes will enable us to plan our strategy and deploy our forces correctly and to work harder for rapid change. Only in this way, moreover, can we encourage people to learn from others willingly so that China can speedily master the world's latest science and technology.

Backwardness must be recognized before it can be changed. One must learn from those who are more advanced before he can catch up with and surpass them. Of course, in order to raise China's scientific and technological level we must rely on our own efforts, develop our own creativity and persist in the policy of independence and self-reliance. But independence does not mean shutting the door on the world, nor does self-reliance mean blind opposition to everything foreign. Science and technology are part of the wealth created in common by all mankind. Every people or country should learn from the advanced science and technology of others. It is not just today, when we are scientifically and technologically backward, that we need to learn from others. Even after we catch up with the most advanced countries, we shall still have to learn from them in areas where they are particularly strong.

China's revolution exerts an attraction on all the revolutionary people in the world, who identify with it. Our drive for socialist modernization has enlisted their interest and support and will continue to do so ever more widely. We must endeavour to increase international academic exchanges and expand our friendly contacts and co-operation with scientific circles in other countries. We would like to express our heartfelt thanks to all friends abroad who have helped us in science and technology.

That was the first question I wanted to speak about.

The second question is that of building a large contingent of scientific and technical personnel who are both "red and expert".

For the modernization of science and technology, we must have a mighty scientific and technical force serving the working class, a force which is both "red and expert" and includes a large number of scientists, engineers and technicians who are first rate by world standards. It will not be easy for us to build up such a force.

Here the important thing is to correctly understand what is meant by both "red and expert" and set reasonable standards.

The Gang of Four made the absurd claim that the more a person knew, the more reactionary he would become. They said they preferred labourers without culture and they touted an ignorant reactionary clown who handed in a blank examination paper as the model of a "red expert". On the other hand, they vilified as "white and expert" those good comrades who studied diligently and contributed to the motherland's science and technology. For a time, this reversal of right and wrong and confounding of the people with the enemy caused deep confusion in many minds.

Comrade Mao Zedong urged intellectuals to become both "red and expert" and encouraged persons with a bourgeois world outlook to remould it and acquire the proletarian world outlook. The basic question as regards world outlook is whom one is to serve. If a person loves our socialist motherland and is serving socialism and the workers, peasants and soldiers of his own free will and accord, then it should be said that he has begun to acquire a proletarian world outlook. In terms of political standards, he cannot be considered "white" but should be called "red". Our scientific undertakings are an integral part of our socialist cause. Working devotedly for our socialist scientific enterprises and making contributions to them is, of course, a sign that one is expert; in a sense, it is also a sign that one is "red".

Imbued with Mao Zedong Thought, our contingent of scientists and technicians has made truly rapid progress in the last twenty-eight years. The large majority of them love the Party and socialism, are striving to integrate themselves with the workers, peasants and soldiers, and work wholeheartedly and successfully at their jobs. Their faith in the Party and in socialism never wavered, even when Lin Biao and the Gang of Four were persecuting and tormenting intellectuals, and they kept on working in their specialities under extremely difficult conditions. Many showed a high level of political awareness in the struggle against the Gang, and when it was smashed their deep revolutionary enthusiasm was released. They fully support the Central Committee of the Party and are working harder than ever for the four modernizations. These scientists and technicians are invaluable to us. On the whole, they have truly proved that they are both "red and expert", that they are the scientific and technical contingent of our working class.

Naturally this does not mean that these scientists and technicians all have a very high level of consciousness politically and ideologically or that there are no mistakes or defects in their way of thinking, work style or day-to-day work. It does mean that judged by the basic criterion, that of political stand, the overwhelming majority of them are revolutionary intellectuals; they take the stand of the working class and constitute a force our Party can rely on. Of course, they on their part should not be complacent or cease to move forward, but should keep on striving for fresh progress both politically and in their own professions. As for their shortcomings and mistakes, these are matters for education and assistance, to be overcome

Speech at National Conference on Science 47

through criticism and self-criticism. No one is free from shortcomings or exempt from making mistakes. Take people like us, cadres doing political work, veteran cadres who have been in the Party for decades. Don't we also have shortcomings and make errors of one kind or another? Why should we be more demanding of vocational cadres and technical experts than of ourselves? As for scientists and technicians who have undesirable family backgrounds, who made mistakes in the past or whose families and social connections present some problems, we should judge them mainly by their own basic political attitudes, by their actual behaviour and by their contributions to socialist revolution and construction.

There is also a group of scientists and technicians whose bourgeois world outlook has not fundamentally changed or who are still deeply influenced by bourgeois ideology. In the midst of sharp, intense and complicated class struggle they often waver. But as long as they are not opposed to the Party and socialism, we should unite with them and educate them, promote their special skills, respect their work, take an interest in their progress and give them a warm helping hand. Comrade Mao Zedong consistently held that the more people we had in our revolutionary ranks the better, that we should respect those who have knowledge and specialized skills or have made contributions, and that our attitude towards any person who has made mistakes should be, first, to observe and, second, to help him instead of turning away from him. We must earnestly put these teachings of Comrade Mao Zedong into practice.

In our socialist society, everyone should remould himself—not just persons who have not changed their basic stand, but everybody. We should all engage in a continued process of learning and transforming our thinking. We should all study fresh problems, absorb what is new and consciously guard against corrosion by bourgeois ideology. In this way, we will be better able to carry out the glorious and arduous task of building a modern, powerful socialist country.

Scientists and technicians should concentrate their energies on their professional work. When we say that at least five-sixths of their work time should be left free for professional work, this is meant as the minimum requirement. It would be better still if more time were made available. If someone works seven days and seven nights a week to meet the needs of science or production, it shows his lofty and selfless devotion to the cause of socialism. We should commend, encourage and learn from such people. It has been demonstrated countless times that only those who devote themselves heart and soul to their work, who constantly strive for perfection and fear neither hardship nor disappointment can reach the pinnacles of science. We cannot demand that scientists and technicians, or at any rate, the overwhelming majority of them, study stacks of books on political theory, join in numerous social activities and attend many meetings not related to their work. Lin Biao and the Gang of Four frequently attacked scientists and technicians, accusing them of being "divorced from politics" and labelling those who studied diligently to enrich their knowledge and improve their skills as "white and expert". "White" is a political concept. Only those who take a reactionary political stand opposed to the Party and socialism can be called "white". How can one pin the "white" label on a person who studies hard to enrich his knowledge and improve his skills? Scientists and technicians who have flaws of one kind or another in their ideology or their style of work shouldn't be called "white" unless they are against the Party and socialism. How can our scientists and technicians who work diligently at socialist scientific enterprises be accused of being divorced from politics? The cause of socialism calls for a division of labour. So long as they keep to the socialist political stand, comrades who devote their best efforts to their posts in different trades and professions are not divorced from politics at all; on the contrary, their devoted work is a concrete manifestation of their socialist consciousness. A few years ago, Lin Biao and the Gang of Four were making it difficult for workers to do their jobs, for peasants to till the land, for armymen to do their military training, for students to study and for scientists and technicians to improve their professional skills. This has inflicted heavy losses on the socialist cause. Hasn't it been a profound lesson?

While making full use of the abilities of our present scientists and technicians and trying to increase their proficiency, we must also exert ourselves to train new personnel. Owing to the sabotage by Lin Biao and the Gang of Four, there is an age gap in our scientific and technical ranks which makes the training of a younger generation of personnel all the more urgent.

We have a vast pool of talent from which to select and train scientists and technicians. The recent reform in our system of college enrolment has brought to light many fine young people who are both hard-working and talented. We are very happy to see their outstanding accomplishments. Though the Gang of Four ran amok for a time, they failed to extinguish the young people's enthusiasm for study or to crush the teachers' revolutionary determination to educate the next generation for the Party and the people. Today the Central Committee is paying close attention to science and education and laying heavy stress on the training and selection of talented people. We can foresee that a new era will soon open, in which talented people will come to the fore in great numbers like a galaxy of brilliant stars. The future of science lies with our youth. The maturing of the younger generation holds the best hopes for the success of our cause.

General education is basic to the training of scientific and technical personnel. We must carry out the Party's policy on education comprehensively and correctly, put it on the right track and introduce appropriate reforms, so as to ensure both quantitative and qualitative progress. Education is not just the concern of the educational units; Party committees at all levels must treat it as a major issue. Every trade and profession should support it and try to establish its own schools. The people's teachers are gardeners cultivating our revolutionary successors. Their creative labour should be respected by the Party and the people. We must see to it that they have enough time for teaching, and we must make proper arrangements for their political life, working conditions and professional studies. Teachers who make outstanding contributions in pedagogy should be commended and rewarded.

We must place particular stress on nurturing talent and break with routine ways of discovering, selecting and training outstanding people. This was one of the big issues about which the Gang of Four spread utter confusion. Scientists, professors and engineers distinguished for their contributions were labelled "bourgeois academic authorities", and outstanding young and middle-aged scientists and technicians trained by our Party and state were vilified as "shoots of revisionism". We must eradicate for good the pernicious influence of the Gang of Four and take up the major task of producing—as quickly as possible—experts in science and technology who are up to the highest international standards. Comrade Mao Zedong said in the early period of the War of Resistance Against Japan (1937–45) that our Party's fighting capacity would be greatly enhanced and Japanese imperialism more quickly defeated if there were one or two hundred comrades with a grasp of Marxism–Leninism which was systematic rather than fragmentary, and genuine rather than hollow. The revolutionary cause needs outstanding revolutionaries, and our scientific undertakings need outstanding scientists. Our working-class scientists of outstanding talent are born of the people and serve the people. Only a broad mass base can generate the continued flow of talents which can help raise the scientific and cultural level of the Chinese nation as a whole.

The discovery and training of talented people by our scientists and teachers is in itself an achievement and a contribution to the country. The history of science shows us the tremendous importance of discovering genuinely talented persons. Some of the world's scientists look upon the finding and training of new talent as the crowning achievement of a lifetime devoted to science. There is much to be said for this view. A number of contemporary China's outstanding mathematicians were discovered while still young by older mathematicians who helped them mature. Some of the newcomers may have surpassed their teachers in scientific achievement, but that only makes the teachers' contributions all the more precious.

The third question I want to discuss is how to introduce, in our scientific and technical units, the system whereby directors of the research institutes assume overall responsibility for work there under the leadership of the respective Party committees.

The rapid growth of China's science and technology depends on good Party leadership in these fields. Our country has entered a new period of development, and the main focus and the style of the Party's work ought both to change correspondingly. Party committees at various levels should simultaneously attend to class struggle, the stuggle for production, and scientific experiment without neglecting any one of them. We should encourage scientific experiments by the masses themselves so as to generate steady technical progress and new production records. There are several hundred thousand industrial enterprises and several hundred thousand agricultural production brigades in our country. The extensive application of advanced science and technology to industry and agriculture and the greater, faster, better and more economical growth of production can be brought about only if every enterprise and every production brigade does its best to carry out technical transformation and scientific experimentation. But at the same time, we must also try to make the best use of our specialized scientific research institutes. Professional researchers are the mainstay of scientific work. Without a strong contingent of top-flight professionals, it will be difficult to scale the heights of modern science and technology, and also difficult for scientific experimentation by the masses to advance in any sustained way. We must try to combine the efforts of the specialists with those of the masses.

The Central Committee has decided that a system of individual responsibility for technical work should be established in scientific research organizations, and that the directors of institutes should assume overall responsibility under the leadership of the Party committees. These organizational measures will be valuable in strengthening the leading role of the Party committees while giving full scope to the skills and talents of the professionals.

The basic task of our scientific research organizations is to produce results and train talent. They must bring about more and better scientific and technical achievements and train scientific and technical personnel who are both "red and expert". The degree to which the organizations fulfil this basic task should be the main criterion for judging the work of their Party committees. Only when they truly fulfil it can we say that they have done their duty in helping to consolidate the dictatorship of the proletariat and to build socialism.

Much has to be done to accomplish this basic task, but it is impossible for

Party committees to handle everything. We must honestly admit that there are still many things in scientific and technical work that we do not understand. And even if we did, it would still be impossible for the Party committees to handle everything. There must be a division of labour with a system of specific individual responsibility for each post, from top to bottom. This is the only way to ensure order and efficiency in our work. And it is the only way to clearly define each person's duties, to distribute rewards and penalties correctly, to avoid procrastination and evasion of responsibility, and to prevent people from getting in each other's way.

The leadership given by Party committees should be primarily political; that is, they should ensure the correct political orientation of the work of the units concerned, see to it that the party's line, principles and policies are followed and arouse and mobilize the enthusiasm of all concerned. Such leadership should be exercised through planning. Good plans for scientific research must be drawn up, personnel must be carefully evaluated and properly placed, and all forces must be well organized. For the plans to be carried out and for scientific research to advance, it is also necessary to guarantee support services for the scientists and technicians, providing them with proper working conditions. This too is part of the work of the Party committees. I am willing to be your director of support services and to co-operate with the leading comrades of Party committees at various levels to do the job properly.

As far as leadership over scientific and technical work is concerned, we should give the directors and deputy directors of the research organizations a free hand. Party committees should support both Party and non-Party professionals occupying administrative posts and enable them to fulfil their roles by giving them power and responsibility commensurate with their positions. These professionals, like us, are cadres of the Party and the state and we must never treat them as outsiders. Party committees should be acquainted with their work and check up on it, but should not attempt to take it over.

We must give full play to democracy and follow the mass line, trusting the judgement of the scientists and technicians in such matters as the evaluation of scientific papers, the assessment of the competence of professional personnel, the elaboration of plans for scientific research and the evaluation of research results. When views diverge on scholarly questions, we must follow the policy of "letting a hundred schools of thought contend" and encourage free discussion. In scientific and technical work, we must listen closely to the opinions of the experts and leave them free to use all their skills and talents so as to achieve better results and reduce our errors to the minimum. This is a vital aspect of the application of the mass line by the Party committees in scientific research organizations.

Will our insistence on allowing scientists and technicians to concentrate on their professional work make our political tasks lighter or less demanding? No, it will not. It will require us to raise the level of our political work, improve our methods, discard formalism, eliminate the pernicious influence of the Gang of Four and learn conscientiously from the fine traditions of political work in the People's Liberation Army. We must support all demands and suggestions that will further scientific work in our socialist society. And we must criticize and educate those who pursue personal gain, who refuse to share their findings or to work in co-operation with others, who try to monopolize information, who plagiarize the work of others or whose ideas and styles of work are detrimental in any other way. Since we are engaged in socialist modernization and are advancing towards the mastery of modern science and technology, a key task in our current political work is to ensure that all scientists and technicians understand how their work relates to the grand goal of the four modernizations. They must be mobilized to collaborate in a revolutionary spirit and with one heart and mind so as to storm the citadels of science.

Although our Party has accumulated some experience in giving leadership to scientific and technical work for over twenty years, we must admit that we are still to a large extent in the "kingdom of necessity", that is, prisoners of our ignorance of the work concerned, and have much to learn about organizing, managing and guiding it effectively. Until this state of affairs changes, it will be difficult for us to score major successes and the initiative will not be in our hands. Comrade Mao Zedong taught us that persons who are in the dark cannot light the way for others. Leading Party cadres at various levels must not be content to remain laymen in science and technology. They must dig in and gradually learn the trade. We must apply ourselves to the study of Marxism and raise our political level, but at the same time we must try to acquire scientific knowledge, to sum up the successes and failures in our work, to study and grasp the objective laws governing scientific and technical work and to implement the Party's principles and policies correctly without neglecting any aspect of them. Just as our Party was able to lead the people in overthrowing the system of exploitation and transforming society, so it will most certainly be able to grasp the laws governing scientific and technical work and lead the people in conquering the heights of world science.

What is right and what is wrong in regard to political line has been basically clarified, we have mapped out a programme and the measures for carrying it out, and the masses are already on the move. The task that now confronts Party organizations at all levels is to inspire real enthusiasm in the masses, to find real solutions to problems and to do really solid work. In a word, we must put everything on a firm footing. We must put a stop to formalism and to the pursuit of appearances without regard for practical results, real efficiency, actual speed, quality or cost. Bad habits like empty talk, boasting and lying must be stamped out.

Comrades,

The Eleventh Party Congress, the First Session of the Fifth National People's Congress and the First Session of the Fifth National Committee of the Chinese People's Political Consultative Conference, which were convened in succession, have fully demonstrated the great unity of our Party and the great unity of the people of all our nationalities. This National Conference on Science is likewise a demonstration of unity. The unity of the Party and the unity of the people—these are the basic guarantees for the triumph of our cause. Let us hold high the great red banner of Mao Zedong Thought and, under the leadership of the Central Committee of the Party, march unswervingly and victoriously towards the grand goal of building a modern and powerful socialist country!

May science flourish and grow! May this conference be a complete success!

Speech at the National Conference on Education
22 April 1978

Comrades,

There have been many new developments on the educational front since the smashing of the Gang of Four and particularly since the college enrolment system was reformed and the "two appraisals" were criticized. These achievements should be fully recognized. Still, both in educational circles and in society at large, people are hoping for even faster progress in this sphere. There are many problems to be solved and many things to be done in this connection. Today, I would like to offer some opinions on the subject.

First, we must improve the quality of education and raise the level of teaching in the sciences, social sciences and humanities so as to serve socialist construction better.

Our schools are places for the training of competent personnel for socialist construction. Are there qualitative standards for such training? Yes, there are. They were stated by Comrade Mao Zedong: We should enable everyone who receives an education to develop morally, intellectually and physically and become a worker possessed of both socialist consciousness and a general education.

The Gang of Four were opposed to placing strict demands on students in their study of the sciences, social sciences and humanities, and to making such studies the main concern of the students. They made the ridiculous claim that that would be "putting intellectual education first" and thus "being divorced from proletarian politics". They declared that they would rather have labourers without education and that the more a person knew, the more reactionary he would become. What is more, they slandered all working people or children of working people who had received some education, calling them "bourgeois intellectuals". Even today, much effort is still needed to eliminate the pernicious influence of these absurdities spread by the Gang.

Lenin emphasized time and again that the workers should not for a minute forget their need for knowledge. Without knowledge, he said, they would have no way of defending themselves, while with it they would be strong. The importance of this truth stands out even more clearly today. We must train workers with a high level of scientific and general knowledge and build a vast army of working-class intellectuals who are both "red and expert". Only then will we be able to master and advance modern science and culture and the new technologies and skills in every trade and profession. Only then will we be able to attain a productivity of labour higher than that under capitalism, transform China into a modern and powerful socialist country and ultimately defeat bourgeois influences in the superstructure. Proletarian politics demands that all these be done.

Beyond all doubt, schools should always attach first importance to a firm and correct political orientation. But this doesn't mean they should devote a great many classroom hours to ideological and political teaching. Students must indeed give top priority to a firm and correct political orientation, but that by no means implies that they should abandon the study of the sciences, social sciences and humanities. On the contrary, the higher the students' political consciousness, the more consciously and diligently they will apply themselves to the study of these subjects for the sake of the revolution. Hence the Gang of Four were not only being utterly ridiculous but were actually negating and betraying proletarian politics when they opposed efforts to improve the quality of education and to raise the students' scientific and cultural level on the basis of a firm, correct political orientation and declared that that was "putting intellectual education first".

It is not good to put too heavy a load on students, and we should continue to take effective measures to prevent this bad practice or remedy it. But it is equally obvious that we will not be able to raise the level of our scientific and cultural knowledge substantially unless we maintain the work style of the "three honests and four stricts",[1] and unless demands are exacting and training rigorous. If we are to catch up with and surpass the advanced countries in science and technology, we must improve not only the quality of our higher education but, first of all, that of our primary and secondary education. In other words, the primary and secondary school courses should be enriched with advanced scientific knowledge, presented in ways the pupils at these levels can understand.

Examinations are a necessary way of checking on the performance of students and teachers, just as the testing of factory products is a necessary

---

[1] "Three honests and four stricts" was a slogan put forward by workers of the Daqing Oilfield in the early 1960s. "Three honests" refers to being an honest person, honest in word and honest in deed in relation to the revolutionary cause. "Four stricts" refers to strict standards, strict organization, a strict attitude and strict discipline in relation to work.

means of quality control. Of course, we must not put blind faith in examinations or consider them the only method for checking up on study. Conscientious research and experimentation are required to improve the form and content of examinations and make them serve their purpose better. Students who don't do well on their examinations should be encouraged and helped to continue their efforts instead of being subjected to unnecessary psychological pressure.

Second, our schools must make an effort to strengthen revolutionary order and discipline, bring up a new generation with socialist consciousness and help to revolutionize the moral tone of our society.

Not only did the sabotage of education by the Gang of Four cause an alarming decline in the quality of scientific and cultural education; it also did grave damage to ideological and political education in the schools, undermined school discipline and sapped the revolutionary spirit of socialist society. The Gang shouted to high heaven about the importance of politics, but in fact their politics were counter-revolutionary and anti-socialist. They used the most decadent and reactionary exploiting-class ideas in their attempt to poison the minds of our young people and turn them into illiterate hooligans. The eradication of the Gang's pernicious influence is a political task which is of the utmost importance and which has a direct bearing on the consolidation of the dictatorship of the proletariat in China.

We should foster revolutionary ideals and communist morality in young people from childhood. This has always been a fine tradition in our Party's educational work. During the years of revolutionary wars, members of the Children's Corps and the Communist Youth League performed stirring deeds of heroism. After Liberation, young people were encouraged to carry on this fine tradition by the schools, the Young Pioneers and the Youth League. For a long time, our children and young people studied well and made progress every day. They were filled with love for their motherland, for the people and for labour, science and public property, and they struggled heroically and resourcefully against bad elements and enemies, setting the tone for a new era. The revolutionary spirit in our schools helped a revolutionary spirit in our whole society. This spirit was unprecedented in Chinese history and won the admiration of people the world over. We hope that not only the comrades working in education and related fields but also every family in our society will pay close attention to the ideological and political progress of our children and young people, so as to revive and enrich the fine revolutionary traditions which the Gang of Four undermined. Comrade Mao Zedong once said: "All departments and organizations should shoulder their responsibilities in ideological and political work. This applies to the Communist Party, the Youth League, government departments in charge of this work, and especially to heads of educational institutions and teachers." The responsibility for training young successors for the revolutionary cause rests particularly heavily on the primary and secondary school teachers and on kindergarten personnel. We should strive to inculcate in our young people the revolutionary style of diligent study, observance of discipline, love of labour, pleasure in helping others, defiance of hardships and courage in the face of the enemy. In this way they can become fine and competent people loyal to the socialist motherland, to the proletarian revolutionary cause and to Marxism–Leninism and Mao Zedong Thought. Thus, when they finish their schooling and take up their jobs, they will be workers imbued with a strong sense of political responsibility and collectivism and a firm revolutionary ideology; their style of work will be to seek truth from facts and follow the mass line, and they will observe strict discipline and work wholeheartedly for the people.

We hope that everyone will do his best to make progress because, when all is said and done, progress depends on individual effort. Collective effort is the sum of individual efforts. And individual effort will continue to differ even in communist society. Comrade Mao Zedong once said that 10,000 years hence there will still be a gap between the advanced and the backward. Therefore, while we encourage and help everyone to do his best, we have to recognize that differences in abilities and character of different people will manifest themselves in the course of their development. We must take these differences into account and do everything possible to enable each individual, in accordance with his particular circumstances, to keep pace with the general movement of society towards socialism and communism. At the same time, conscientious efforts must be made and strict measures taken to correct and reform those who seriously undermine revolutionary order and discipline and refuse to mend their ways after repeated efforts to educate them; in no case should we let a handful of such persons harm our schools and society as a whole.

From now on, it is not only the secondary schools and institutions of higher education that should examine applicants in an overall way—taking into account their moral and intellectual qualities and the state of their health—and admit only those who are best qualified. All units should gradually follow suit and recruit only those job applicants who are best qualified. This will require that students be enabled to develop morally, intellectually and physically and to become workers with both socialist consciousness and a general education. Thus the policy put forward by Comrade Mao Zedong to the same effect will be thoroughly implemented in all aspects of social life. This system of selection will be most useful in raising the political, scientific and cultural levels of our working personnel, in meeting the special needs of different trades and professions, and in creating, among the young people and throughout our society, a revolutionary atmosphere in which everyone is eager to make progress and work hard and is unwilling to lag behind.

Third, education must meet the requirements of our country's economic development.

To train qualified personnel for socialist construction, we must try to find improved ways of combining education with productive labour, ways that are suited to our new conditions. Marx, Engels, Lenin and Comrade Mao Zedong all laid great stress on combining education with productive labour. They considered this to be one of the most powerful means for reforming society under capitalism. They also believed that after the seizure of political power by the proletariat, it should be the fundamental way to train a new generation that would integrate theory with practice, unite study with practical application and develop in an all-round way, and they looked upon it as an essential measure for gradually abolishing the distinction between mental and manual labour. As early as 80 years ago, Lenin said: ". . . Neither training and education without productive labour, nor productive labour without parallel training and education [can] be raised to the degree required by the present level of technology and the state of scientific knowledge." In our own day, rapid economic and technological progress demands rapid improvement in the quality and efficiency of education. This includes steady improvement in the methods of combining study with productive labour and of selecting the type of labour appropriate for this purpose.

To this end, educational institutions of all types and levels must make appropriate decisions as to what kind of labour the students should engage in, which factories and rural areas they should go to and for how long, and how to relate their labour closely to their studies. More important still, education as a whole must be in keeping with the requirements of our growing economy. If, on the contrary, what the students learn isn't suited to the needs of their future jobs, if they study what they aren't going to apply or if they can't apply what they study, won't this flatly violate the principle of combining education with productive labour? And, if that is so, how can we arouse the student's enthusiasm for study and work and how can education meet the enormous demands placed on it by the new historical period?

As our economy develops in a planned and balanced way, we must also carefully plan the training of future workers and professionals to meet its needs. We must bear in mind not only immediate needs but future ones as well. We must make plans that take into full account not only the needs of growing production and construction but also the trends in modern science and technology.

The State Planning Commission, the Ministry of Education and other organizations should collaborate in making education an integral component of the national economic plan. We should co-ordinate the development of various types and levels of educational institutions and, in particular, we should plan to increase the number of agricultural secondary schools and vocational and technical secondary schools. We should also consider what types of institutions of higher learning to build up, how to readjust the specialities offered, how to institute the courses on basic theory and how to improve teaching materials. We must take steps to accelerate the development of modern media of education, including radio and television. Broadcasting offers an important means of developing education with greater, faster, better and more economical results, and we should take full advantage of it. We should study and find ways of co-ordinating productive labour and scientific experiment and research more effectively in our schools so as to better meet the needs of our economic and educational plans. In order to speed up the training of qualified personnel and to raise the overall level of education, we must consider concentrating our forces and strengthening key colleges and universities and key primary and secondary schools, thus raising their level as quickly as possible.

From now on, the state will be trying to open up new productive enterprises and new lines of work so as to serve the four modernizations more effectively. In working out our educational plan, we should co-ordinate it with the state plan for the utilization of labour and consider how to meet the needs for increased employment.

Lastly, I would like to say a few words about ensuring respect for the labour of our teachers and about improving their qualifications.

Teachers are the key to a school's success in training personnel suited to the needs of our socialist construction, that is, its success in training workers who have both socialist consciousness and a good general education and who are highly developed morally, intellectually and physically.

In the past two decades and more, we have built up a contingent of nine million teachers devoted to serving the people. The overwhelming majority of teachers and other school personnel love the Party and socialism. They work industriously to provide a socialist education and so have made great contributions to the nation and the proletariat. Educational workers who serve the people are high-minded workers for the revolution. We salute this multitude of educational workers for their painstaking efforts and express our appreciation to all of them and especially to the primary school teachers, who have worked tirelessly under particularly difficult conditions to bring up successors for the revolutionary cause.

We must raise the political and social status of teachers. They should command the respect not only of their students but also of the whole community. We urge students to respect their teachers and teachers to love their students. Respect and love, with teacher and student learning from each other—that is the appropriate comradely, revolutionary relationship between teachers and students. Outstanding educational workers should be commended, rewarded and widely acclaimed.

The present pay scale for teachers, especially those in primary and secondary schools, should be reviewed. Proper steps should be taken to encourage people to dedicate their whole lives to education. Particularly outstanding teachers may be designated "special-grade teachers". Owing to our country's economic limitations, we cannot bring about a marked improvement in the material life of teachers and other school personnel for the time being, but we must make every effort to create the conditions needed for this. The Party committees at all levels and the administrative authorities in charge of education should, first of all, do everything possible to provide better collective welfare services.

All Party committees and Party organizations in the schools should take a warm interest in the teachers' ideological and political progress. They should help the teachers to study Marxism–Leninism and Mao Zedong Thought so that more of them will have a firm proletarian, communist world outlook. We must make a point of recruiting outstanding teachers into the Party. The tasks of education are becoming heavier and heavier. All educational units must strive to raise the capabilities of teachers and improve the quality of instruction. The Ministry of Education and local educational departments should adopt effective measures to train teachers, making full use of radio and television, setting up training classes and advanced courses of various kinds, compiling reference material for teachers, and so forth. We hope that all teachers will work hard to steadily raise their political and professional levels and become increasingly socialist-minded and professionally competent.

Comrades!

I hope that some of the major issues in educational work will be fully discussed at this conference. We urge you to proceed in the revolutionary spirit of daring to think and speak. It doesn't matter if opinions differ. We can compare the different proposals. We must follow the mass line in everything we do. Good ideas can be produced only if democracy is practised fully within the ranks of the people. Of course, a good idea will not turn into reality by itself. Bright prospects remain merely idle talk unless we devise practical measures and work hard to implement them. If we are to achieve the four modernizations within a reasonable length of time, we must insist on a practical, revolutionary style of work that will gradually help us turn lofty ideals into reality.

I believe that if—under the leadership of the Central Committee of the Party—we rely on the efforts of the teachers, students, administrators and other school workers, carry through to the end the struggle to expose and criticize the Gang of Four, and approach our work in a practical way, we will see more and more people of a new type emerge. Good news will pour in from the educational front as our work in this domain thrives the way it is doing in all others.

Emancipate the Mind, Seek Truth from Facts and Unite as One in Looking to the Future*
13 December 1978

Comrades,

This conference has lasted over a month and will soon end. The Central Committee has put forward the fundamental guiding principle of shifting the focus of all Party work to the four modernizations and has solved a host of important problems inherited from the past. This will surely strengthen the determination, confidence and unity of the Party, the army and the people of all of China's nationalities. Now we can be certain that under the correct leadership of the Central Committee, the Party, army and people will achieve victory after victory in our new Long March.

The present conference has been very successful and will have an important place in our Party's history. We have not held one like it for many years. There has been lively debate here and the Party's democratic tradition has been revived and carried forward. We should spread this style of work to the whole Party, army and people.

At this conference we have discussed and resolved many major issues concerning the destinies of our Party and state. The participants have spoken their minds freely and fully and have boldly aired their honest opinions. They have laid problems on the table and have felt free to criticize things, including the work of the Central Committee. Some comrades have criticized themselves to varying degrees. All this represents marked progress in our inner-Party life and will give a big impetus to the cause of our Party and people.

---

*Speech at the closing session of the Central Working Conference which made preparations for the Third Plenary Session of the Eleventh Central Committee of the Chinese Communist Party that immediately followed. In essence, this speech served as the keynote address for the Third Plenary Session.

Emancipate the Mind

Today, I mainly want to discuss one question, namely, how to emancipate our minds, use our heads, seek truth from facts and unite as one in looking to the future.

I. EMANCIPATING THE MIND IS A VITAL POLITICAL TASK

When it comes to emancipating our minds, using our heads, seeking truth from facts and uniting as one in looking to the future, the primary task is to emancipate our minds. Only then can we, guided as we should be by Marxism–Leninism and Mao Zedong Thought, find correct solutions to the emerging as well as inherited problems, fruitfully reform those aspects of the relations of production and of the superstructure that do not correspond with the rapid development of our productive forces, and chart the specific course and formulate the specific policies, methods and measures needed to achieve the four modernizations under our actual conditions.

The emancipation of minds has not been completely achieved among our cadres, particularly our leading cadres. Indeed, many comrades have not yet set their brains going; in other words, their ideas remain rigid or partly so. That isn't because they are not good comrades. It is a result of specific historical conditions.

First, it is because during the past dozen years Lin Biao and the Gang of Four set up ideological taboos or "forbidden zones" and preached blind faith to confine people's minds within the framework of their phoney Marxism. No one was allowed to go beyond the limits they prescribed; anyone who did was tracked down, stigmatized and attacked politically. In this situation, some people found it safer to stop using their heads and thinking questions over.

Second, it is because democratic centralism was undermined and the Party was afflicted with bureaucratism resulting from, among other things, over-concentration of power. This kind of bureaucratism often masquerades as "Party leadership", "Party directives", "Party interests" and "Party discipline", but actually it is designed to control people, hold them in check and oppress them. At that time many important issues were often decided by one or two persons. The others could only do what those few ordered. That being so, there wasn't much point in thinking things out for yourself.

Third, it is because no clear distinction was made between right and wrong or between merit and demerit, and because rewards and penalties were not meted out as deserved. No distinction was made between those who worked well and those who didn't. In some cases, even people who worked well were attacked while those who did nothing or just played it safe weathered every storm. Under those unwritten laws, people were naturally reluctant to use their brains.

Fourth, it is because people are still subject to the force of habit of the small producer, who sticks to old conventions, is content with the status quo and is unwilling to seek progress or accept anything new.

When people's minds aren't yet emancipated and their thinking remains rigid, curious phenomena emerge.

Once people's thinking becomes rigid, they will increasingly act according to fixed notions. To cite some examples, strengthening Party leadership is interpreted as the Party's monopolizing and interfering in everything. Exercising centralized leadership is interpreted as erasing distinctions between the Party and the government, so that the former replaces the latter. And maintaining unified leadership by the Central Committee is interpreted as "doing everything according to unified standards". We are opposed to "home-grown policies" that violate the fundamental principles of those laid down by the Central Committee, but there are also "home-grown policies" that are truly grounded in reality and supported by the masses. Yet such correct policies are still often denounced for their "not conforming to the unified standards".

People whose thinking has become rigid tend to veer with the wind. They are not guided by Party spirit and Party principles, but go along with whatever has the backing of the authorities and adjust their words and actions according to whichever way the wind is blowing. They think that they will thus avoid mistakes. In fact, however, veering with the wind is in itself a grave mistake, a contravention of the Party spirit which all Communists should cherish. It is true that people who think independently and dare to speak out and act can't avoid making mistakes, but their mistakes are out in the open and are therefore more easily rectified.

Once people's thinking becomes rigid, book worship, divorced from reality, becomes a grave malady. Those who suffer from it dare not say a word or take a step that isn't mentioned in books, documents or the speeches of leaders: everything has to be copied. Thus responsibility to the higher authorities is set in opposition to responsibility to the people.

Our drive for the four modernizations will get nowhere unless rigid thinking is broken down and the minds of cadres and of the masses are completely emancipated.

In fact, the current debate about whether practice is the sole criterion for testing truth is also a debate about whether people's minds need to be emancipated. Everybody has recognized that this debate is highly important and necessary. Its importance is becoming clearer all the time.

When everything has to be done by the book, when thinking turns rigid and blind faith is the fashion, it is impossible for a party or a nation to make progress. Its life will cease and that party or nation will perish. Comrade Mao Zedong said this time and again during the rectification movements. Only if we emancipate our minds, seek truth from facts, proceed from reality in everything and integrate theory with practice, can we carry out our socialist modernization programme smoothly, and only then can our Party further develop Marxism–Leninism and Mao Zedong Thought. In this sense, the debate about the criterion for testing truth is really a debate about ideological line, about politics, about the future and the destiny of our Party and nation.

Seeking truth from facts is the basis of the proletarian world outlook as well as the ideological basis of Marxism. Just as in the past we achieved all the victories in our revolution by following this principle, so today we must rely on it in our effort to accomplish the four modernizations. Comrades in every factory, government office, school, shop and production team as well as comrades in Party committees at the central, provincial, prefectural, county and commune levels — all should act on this principle, emancipate their minds and use their heads in thinking questions through and taking action on them.

The more Party members and other people there are who use their heads and think things through, the more our cause will benefit. To make revolution and build socialism we need large numbers of pathbreakers who dare to think, explore new ways and generate new ideas. Otherwise, we won't be able to rid our country of poverty and backwardness or to catch up with — still less surpass — the advanced countries. We hope every Party committee and every Party branch will encourage and support people both inside and outside the Party to dare to think, explore new paths and put forward new ideas, and that they will urge the masses to emancipate their minds and use their heads.

II. DEMOCRACY IS A MAJOR CONDITION FOR EMANCIPATING THE MIND

One important condition for getting people to emancipate their minds and use their heads is genuine practice of the proletarian system of democratic centralism. We need unified and centralized leadership, but centralism can be correct only when there is a full measure of democracy.

At present, we must lay particular stress on democracy, because for quite a long time democratic centralism was not genuinely practised: centralism was divorced from democracy and there was too little democracy. Even today, only a few advanced people dare to speak up. There are a good many such people at this conference. But in the Party and the country as a whole, there are still many who hesitate to speak their minds. Even when they have worthwhile opinions, they hesitate to express them, and they are not bold enough in struggling against bad things and bad people. If this doesn't change, how can we persuade everyone to emancipate his mind and use his head? And how can we bring about the four modernizations?

We must create the conditions for the practice of democracy, and for this it is essential to reaffirm the principle of the "three don'ts": don't pick on others for their faults, don't put labels on people, and don't use a big stick. In political life within the Party and among the people we must use democratic means and not resort to coercion or attack. The rights of citizens, Party members and Party committee members are respectively stipulated by the Constitution of the People's Republic and the Constitution of the Communist Party. These rights must be resolutely defended and no infringement of them must be allowed.

The recent reversal of the verdict on the Tiananmen Incident has elated the people of all of China's nationalities and greatly stimulated mass enthusiasm for socialism. The masses should be encouraged to offer criticisms. There is nothing to worry about even if a few malcontents take advantage of democracy to make trouble. We should deal with such situations appropriately, having faith that the overwhelming majority of the people are able to use their own judgement. One thing a revolutionary party does need to worry about is its inability to hear the voice of the people. The thing to be feared most is silence. Today many rumours — some true, some false — circulate through the grapevine inside and outside the Party. This is a kind of punishment for the long-standing lack of political democracy. If we had a political situation with both centralism and democracy, both discipline and freedom, both unity of will and personal ease of mind and liveliness, there wouldn't be so many rumours and anarchism would be easier to overcome. We believe our people are mindful of the overall interests of the country and have a good sense of discipline. Our leading cadres at all levels, and especially those of high rank, should for their part take care to strictly observe Party discipline and keep Party secrets; they should refrain from spreading rumours, circulating handwritten copies of speeches and the like.

As it is only natural that some opinions expressed by the masses should be correct and others not, we should examine them analytically. The Party leadership should be good at synthesizing the correct opinions and explaining why the others are incorrect. In dealing with ideological problems we must never use coercion but should genuinely carry out the policy of "letting a hundred flowers bloom, a hundred schools of thought contend". We must firmly put a stop to bad practices such as attacking and trying to silence people who make critical comments — especially sharp ones — by ferreting out their political backgrounds, tracing political rumours to them and opening "special case" files on them. Comrade Mao Zedong used to say that such actions were really signs of weakness and lack of courage. No leading comrades at any level must ever place themselves in opposition to the masses. We must never abandon this principle. But of course we must not let down our guard against the handful of counter-revolutionaries who still exist in our country.

Now I want to speak at some length about economic democracy. Under our present system of economic management, power is over-concentrated, so it is necessary to devolve some of it to the lower levels without hesitation but in a planned way. Otherwise it will be difficult to give full scope to the initiative of local as well as national authorities and to the enterprises and workers, and difficult to practise modern economic management and raise the productivity of labour. The various localities, enterprises and production teams should be given greater powers of decision regarding both operation and management. There are many provinces, municipalities and autonomous regions in China, and some of our medium-sized provinces are as big as a large European country. They must be given greater powers of decision in economic planning, finance and foreign trade — always within the framework of a nationwide unity of views, policies, planning, guidance and action.

At present the most pressing need is to expand the decision-making powers of mines, factories and other enterprises and of production teams, so as to give full scope to their initiative and creativity. Once a production team has been empowered to make decisions regarding its own operations, its members and cadres will lie awake at night so long as a single piece of land is left unplanted or a single pond unused for aquatic production, and they will find ways to remedy the situation. Just imagine the additional wealth that could be created if all the people in China's hundreds of thousands of enterprises and millions of production teams put their minds to work. As more wealth is created for the state, personal income and collective benefits should also be increased somewhat. As far as the relatively small number of advanced people is concerned, it won't matter too much if we neglect the principle of more pay for more work and fail to stress individual material benefits. But when it comes to the masses, that approach can only be used for a short time — it won't work in the long run. Revolutionary spirit is a treasure beyond price. Without it there would be no revolutionary action. But revolution takes place on the basis of the need for material benefit. It would be idealism to emphasize the spirit of sacrifice to the neglect of material benefit.

It is also essential to ensure the democratic rights of the workers and peasants, including the rights of democratic election, management and supervision. We must create a situation in which not only every workshop director and production team leader but also every worker and peasant is aware of his responsibility for production and tries to find ways of solving related problems.

To ensure people's democracy, we must strengthen our legal system. Democracy has to be institutionalized and written into law, so as to make sure that institutions and laws do not change whenever the leadership changes, or whenever the leaders change their views or shift the focus of their attention. The trouble now is that our legal system is incomplete, with many laws yet to be enacted. Very often, what leaders say is taken as the law and anyone who disagrees is called a law-breaker. That kind of law changes whenever a leader's views change. So we must concentrate on enacting criminal and civil codes, procedural laws and other necessary laws concerning factories, people's communes, forests, grasslands and environmental protection, as well as labour laws and a law on investment by foreigners. These laws should be discussed and adopted through democratic procedures. Meanwhile, the procuratorial and judicial organs should be strengthened. All this will ensure that there are laws to go by, that they are observed and strictly enforced, and that violators are brought to book. The relations between one enterprise and another, between enterprises and the state, between enterprises and individuals, and so on should also be defined by law, and many of the contradictions between them should be resolved by law. There is a lot of legislative work to do, and we don't have enough trained people. Therefore, legal provisions will have to be less than perfect to start with, then be gradually improved upon. Some laws and statutes can be tried out in particular localities and later enacted nationally after the experience has been evaluated and improvements have been made. Individual legal provisions can be revised or supplemented one at a time, as necessary; there is no need to wait for a comprehensive revision of an entire body of law. In short, it is better to have some laws than none, and better to have them sooner than later. Moreover, we should intensify our study of international law.

Just as the country must have laws, the Party must have rules and regulations. The fundamental ones are embodied in the Party Constitution. Without rules and regulations in the Party it would be hard to ensure that the laws of the state are enforced. The task of the Party's discipline inspection commissions and its organization departments at all levels is not only to deal with particular cases but, more important, to uphold the Party's rules and regulations and make earnest efforts to improve its style of work. Disciplinary measures should be taken against all persons who violate Party discipline, no matter who they are, so that clear differentiation is made between merits and demerits, rewards and penalties are meted out as deserved, and rectitude prevails and bad tendencies are stemmed.

III. SOLVING OLD PROBLEMS WILL HELP PEOPLE LOOK TO THE FUTURE

This conference has solved some problems left over from the past and distinguished clearly between the merits and demerits of some persons, and remedies have been made for a number of major cases in which the charges were false or which were unjustly or incorrectly dealt with. This is essential for emancipating minds and for ensuring political stability and unity. Its purpose is to help us turn our thoughts to the future and smoothly shift the focus of the Party's work.

Our principle is that every wrong should be righted. All wrongs done in the past should be corrected. Some questions that cannot be settled right now should be settled after this conference. But settlement must be prompt and effective, without leaving any loose ends and on the basis of facts. We must solve these problems left over from the past thoroughly. It is not good for them to be left unsolved or for comrades who have made mistakes to refuse to make self-criticisms, or for us to fail to deal with their cases properly. However, we cannot possibly achieve — and should not expect — a perfect settlement of every case. We should have the major aspect of each problem in mind and solve it in broad outline; to go into every detail is neither possible nor necessary.

Stability and unity are of prime importance. To strengthen the unity of people of whatever nationality, we must first strengthen unity throughout the Party, and especially within the central leadership. Our Party's unity is based on Marxism–Leninism and Mao Zedong Thought. Inside the Party we should distinguish right from wrong in terms of theory and of the Party line, conduct criticism and self-criticism and help and supervise each other in correcting wrong ideas.

Comrades who have made mistakes should be urged to sum up their experience and draw the necessary lessons, so that they can recognize those mistakes and correct them. We should give them time to think. Once they improve their understanding of cardinal issues of right and wrong and conduct self-criticism, we should make them welcome again. In dealing with people who have made mistakes, we must weigh each case very carefully. Where there is a choice, it is better to err on the side of leniency, but we should be more severe if the problems recur. We should be somewhat lenient with rank-and-file Party members, but more severe with leading cadres, especially those of high rank.

From now on we must be very careful in the selection of cadres. We must never assign important posts to persons who have engaged in beating, smashing and looting, who have been obsessed by factionalist ideas, who have sold their souls by framing innocent comrades, or who disregard the Party's vital interests. Nor can we lightly trust persons who sail with the wind, curry favour with those in power and ignore the Party's principles. We should be wary of such people and at the same time educate them and urge them to change their world outlook.

People both at home and abroad have been greatly concerned recently about how we would evaluate Comrade Mao Zedong and the Cultural Revolution. The great contributions of Comrade Mao in the course of long revolutionary struggles will never fade. If we look back at the years following the failure of the revolution in 1927, it appears very likely that without his outstanding leadership the Chinese revolution would still not have triumphed even today. In that case, the people of all our nationalities would still be suffering under the reactionary rule of imperialism, feudalism and bureaucrat-capitalism, and our Party would still be engaged in bitter struggle in the dark. Therefore, it is no exaggeration to say that were it not for Chairman Mao there would be no New China. Mao Zedong Thought has nurtured our whole generation. All comrades present here may be said to have been nourished by Mao Zedong Thought. Without Mao Zedong Thought, the Communist Party of China would not exist today, and that is no exaggeration either. Mao Zedong Thought will forever remain the greatest intellectual treasure of our Party, our army and our people. We must understand the scientific tenets of Mao Zedong Thought correctly and as an integral whole and develop them under the new historical conditions. Of course Comrade Mao was not infallible or free from shortcomings. To demand that of any revolutionary leader would be inconsistent with Marxism. We must guide and educate the Party members, the army officers and men and the people of all of China's nationalities and help them to see the great services of Comrade Mao Zedong scientifically and in historical perspective.

The Cultural Revolution should also be viewed scientifically and in historical perspective. In initiating it Comrade Mao Zedong was actuated mainly by the desire to oppose and prevent revisionism. As for the shortcomings that appeared during the course of the Cultural Revolution and the mistakes that were made then, at an appropriate time they should be summed up and lessons should be drawn from them — that is essential for achieving unity of understanding throughout the Party. The Cultural Revolution has become a stage in the course of China's socialist development, hence we must evaluate it. However, there is no need to do so hastily. Serious research must be done before we can make a scientific

Emancipate the Mind 71

appraisal of this historical stage. It may take a rather long time to fully understand and assess some of the particular issues involved. We will probably be able to make a more correct analysis of this period in history after some time has passed than we can right now.

IV. STUDY THE NEW SITUATION AND TACKLE THE NEW PROBLEMS

In order to look forward, we must study the new situation and tackle the new problems in good time; otherwise, there can be no smooth progress. In three fields especially, the new situation and new problems demand attention: methods of management, structure of management and economic policy.

So far as methods of management are concerned, we should lay particular stress on overcoming bureaucratism.

Our bureaucracy, which is a result of small-scale production, is utterly incompatible with large-scale production. To achieve the four modernizations and shift the technological basis of our entire socialist economy to that of large-scale production, it is essential to overcome the evils of bureaucracy. Our present economic management is marked by overstaffing, organizational overlapping, complicated procedures and extremely low efficiency. Everything is often drowned in empty political talk. This is not the fault of any group of comrades. The fault lies in the fact that we haven't made reforms in time. Our modernization programme and socialist cause will be doomed if we don't make them now.

We must learn to manage the economy by economic means. If we ourselves don't know about advanced methods of management, we should learn from those who do, either at home or abroad. These methods should be applied not only in the operation of enterprises with newly imported technology and equipment, but also in the technical transformation of existing enterprises. Pending the introduction of a unified national programme of modern management, we can begin with limited spheres, say, a particular region or a given trade, and then spread the methods gradually to others. The central government departments concerned should encourage such experiments. Contradictions of all kinds will crop up in the process and we should discover and overcome them in good time. That will speed up our progress.

Henceforth, now that the question of political line has been settled, the quality of leadership given by the Party committee in an economic unit should be judged mainly by the unit's adoption of advanced methods of management, by the progress of its technical innovation, and by the margins of increase of its productivity of labour, its profits, the personal income of its workers and the collective benefits it provides. The quality of leadership by Party committees in all fields should be judged by similar criteria. This will be of major political importance in the years to come. Without these criteria as its key elements, our politics would be empty and divorced from the highest interests of both the Party and the people.

So far as the structure of management is concerned, the most important task at present is to strengthen the work responsibility system.

Right now a big problem in enterprises and institutions across the country and in Party and government organs at various levels is that nobody takes responsibility. In theory, there is collective responsibility. In fact, this means that no one is responsible. When a task is assigned, nobody sees that it is properly fulfilled or cares whether the result is satisfactory. So there is an urgent need to establish a strict reponsibility system. Lenin said, "To refer to collegiate methods as an excuse for irresponsibility is a most dangerous evil." He called it "an evil which must be halted at all costs as quickly as possible and by whatever the means".

For every job or construction project it is necessary to specify the work to be done, the personnel required to do it, work quotas, standards of quality, and a time schedule. For example, in introducing foreign technology and equipment we should specify what items are to be imported from where, where they are going, and who is to take charge of the work. Whether it is a question of importing foreign equipment or of operating an existing enterprise, similar specifications should be made. When problems arise, it doesn't help just to blame the planning commissions and Party committees concerned, as we do now — the particular persons responsible must feel the heat. By the same token, rewards also should go to specific collectives and persons. In implementing the system according to which the factory directors assume overall responsibility under the leadership of the Party committees, we must state explicitly who is responsible for each aspect of the work.

To make the best use of the responsibility system the following measures are essential.

First, we must extend the authority of the managerial personnel. Whoever is given responsibility should be given authority as well. Whoever it is — a factory director, engineer, technician, accountant or cashier — he should have his own area not only of responsibility but of authority, which must not be infringed upon by others. The responsibility system is bound to fail if there is only responsibility without authority.

Second, we must select personnel wisely and assign duties according to ability. We should seek out existing specialists and train new ones, put them in important positions, raise their political status and increase their material benefits. What are the political requirements in selecting someone for a job? The major criterion is whether the person chosen can work for the good of the people and contribute to the development of the productive forces and to the socialist cause as a whole.

Third, we must have a strict system of evaluation and distinguish clearly between a performance that should be rewarded and one that should be penalized. All enterprises, schools, research institutes and government offices should set up systems for evaluating work and conferring academic, technical and honorary titles. Rewards and penalties, promotions and demotions should be based on work performance. And they should be linked to increases or reductions in material benefits.

In short, through strengthening the responsibility system and allotting rewards and penalties fairly, we should create an atmosphere of friendly emulation in which people vie with one another to become advanced elements, working hard and aiming high.

In economic policy, I think we should allow some regions and enterprises and some workers and peasants to earn more and enjoy more benefits sooner than others, in accordance with their hard work and greater contributions to society. If the standard of living of some people is raised first, this will inevitably be an impressive example to their "neighbours", and people in other regions and units will want to learn from them. This will help the whole national economy to advance wave upon wave and help the people of all our nationalities to become prosperous in a comparatively short period.

Of course, there are still difficulties in production in the Northwest, Southwest and some other regions, and the life of the people there is hard. The state should give these places many kinds of help, and in particular strong material support.

These are major policies which can have an effect on the whole national economy and push it forward. I suggest that you study them carefully.

During the drive to realize the four modernizations, we are bound to encounter many new and unexpected situations and problems with which we are unfamiliar. In particular, the reforms in the relations of production and in the superstructure will not be easy to introduce. They touch on a wide range of issues and concern the immediate interests of large numbers of people, so they are bound to give rise to complications and problems and to meet with numerous obstacles. In the reorganization of enterprises, for example, there will be the problem of deciding who will stay on and who will leave, while in that of government departments, a good many people will be transferred to other jobs, and some may complain. And so on. Since we will have to confront such problems soon, we must be mentally prepared for them. We must teach Party members and the masses to give top priority to the overall situation and the overall interests of the Party and the state. We should be full of confidence. We will be able to solve any problem and surmount any obstacle so long as we have faith in the masses, follow the mass line and explain the situation and problems to them. There can be no doubt that as the economy grows, more and more possibilities will open up and each person will be able to make his contribution to society.

The four modernizations represent a great and profound revolution in which we are moving forward by resolving one new contradiction after another. Therefore, all Party comrades must learn well and always keep on learning.

On the eve of nationwide victory in the Chinese revolution, Comrade Mao Zedong called on the whole Party to start learning afresh. We did that pretty well and consequently, after entering the cities, we were able to rehabilitate the economy very quickly and then to accomplish the socialist transformation. But we must admit that we have not learned well enough in the subsequent years. Expending our main efforts on political campaigns, we did not master the skills needed to build our country. Our socialist construction failed to progress satisfactorily and we experienced grave setbacks politically. Now that our task is to achieve modernization, our lack of the necessary knowledge is even more obvious. So the whole Party must start learning again.

What shall we learn? Basically, we should study Marxism–Leninism and Mao Zedong Thought and try to integrate the universal principles of Marxism with the concrete practice of our modernization drive. At present most of our cadres need also to apply themselves to three subjects: economics, science and technology, and management. Only if we study these well will we be able to carry out socialist modernization rapidly and efficiently. We should learn in different ways — through practice, from books and from the experience, both positive and negative, of others as well as our own. Conservatism and book worship should be overcome. The several hundred members and alternate members of the Central Committee and the thousands of senior cadres at the central and local levels should take the lead in making an in-depth study of modern economic development.

So long as we unite as one, work in concert, emancipate our minds, use our heads and try to learn what we did not know before, there is no doubt that we will be able to quicken the pace of our new Long March. Under the leadership of the Central Committee and the State Council, let us advance courageously to change the backward condition of our country and turn it into a modern and powerful socialist state.

The United Front and the Tasks of the Chinese People's Political Consultative Conference in the New Period

15 June 1979

Fellow Committee Members and Comrades,

The Second Session of the Fifth National Committee of the Chinese People's Political Consultative Conference is now open.

It is convening after the decision by the Central Committee of the Communist Party of China to shift the focus of the work of our Party and state to socialist modernization. Accordingly, its goal is to further mobilize and unite the people of all nationalities in China and all patriotic forces in our country so as to promote socialist modernization.

This year marks the thirtieth anniversary of the founding both of the great People's Republic of China and of the Chinese People's Political Consultative Conference. China has now entered a new historical period in which the central task is to achieve the four modernizations. Our revolutionary united front has likewise entered a new historical period in its development.

During these three decades, the class situation in Chinese society has changed fundamentally. The position of our working class has been enormously strengthened, and our peasants have been members of collectives for more than twenty years. The worker–peasant alliance will be further consolidated and developed on the new basis of socialist modernization. Chinese intellectuals, including the overwhelming majority of the old intellectuals from pre-Liberation society, have become part of the working class and now serve the cause of socialism consciously and actively.

Through democratic reform and socialist transformation, all fraternal nationalities in China one after another have long since taken the socialist road, and they have formed a new, socialist type of relationship among themselves—a relationship of unity, fraternity, mutual assistance and co-operation. China's patriots, whatever their nationality and religion, have made considerable progress along this road. In the course of bringing about the four modernizations, the nationalities will achieve an even greater degree of socialist unanimity and their unity will become stronger and stronger.

The means of production formerly owned by the Chinese capitalist class came under state control long ago, and the payment of a fixed rate of interest ended thirteen years ago. The overwhelming majority of the capitalists with the capacity to work have transformed themselves into working people who earn their own living in our socialist society. Our successful completion of the socialist transformation of capitalist industry and commerce is one of the most brilliant victories in the history of socialism in China and indeed in the world. It was won because the Chinese Communist Party led our country's working class in implementing the Marxist policies formulated by Comrade Mao Zedong in the light of China's specific conditions, and because most members of the capitalist class, especially the progressives among them, played a positive, co-operative role in accepting this transformation. Today, as working people, they are contributing their share to our socialist modernization.

China's democratic parties have a glorious history in the democratic revolution and they also performed notable services during the socialist transformation. This the Chinese people will never forget. Now all these parties have become political alliances of those socialist working people and those patriots supporting socialism with whom these parties are respectively linked. All are political forces that serve socialism under the leadership of the Chinese Communist Party.

The thoughts of our compatriots in Taiwan, Xianggang (Hongkong) and Aomen (Macao) and of Chinese nationals overseas turn with longing to the motherland, and their sense of patriotism has grown constantly stronger. They are playing an increasingly important and positive part in the effort to achieve the great goal of reunifying our motherland, in supporting the country's modernization and in strengthening the international struggle against hegemonism.

All these changes demonstrate that China's united front has become a broad alliance of socialist working people and patriots supporting socialism, led by the working class and based on the worker–peasant alliance. The tasks of the united front and of the CPPCC in the new period are to mobilize all positive forces, strive to transform all negative forces into positive ones, and unite with all the forces that can be united so that all can work in harmony to maintain and strengthen political stability and unity in China and make it a modern, powerful socialist country.

To realize the four modernizations, it is essential to promote socialist democracy and strengthen the socialist legal system. The CPPCC is an important organization for promoting people's democracy and maintaining contacts with people in different walks of life. To achieve China's socialist modernization it continues to be necessary for the participants in the CPPCC to hold consultations and discussions on the nation's general principles, its political life and the social and economic questions related to modernization. It is still necessary for them to exercise supervision over each other and over the enforcement of the Constitution and law. We must give scope to the free airing of views and make full use of all talents. We must uphold the principle of the "three don'ts": don't pick on others for their faults, don't put labels on people, and don't use a big stick. And we must encourage the full expression of opinions, demands, criticisms and suggestions from all quarters, so that the government can benefit from them, promptly discover and correct its own shortcomings and mistakes and push forward all phases of our work.

To achieve the four modernizations, it is essential that we strengthen the ideological and political education of the whole people, while maintaining the proletarian dictatorship over the handful of anti-socialist elements. The CPPCC will undoubtedly continue to perform a very useful role in this work. The united front and the CPPCC should carry forward the tradition of self-education and self-remoulding, continue ideological remoulding in accordance with the formula "unity—criticism—unity", and help the masses and prominent individuals in various spheres to constantly strengthen unity and make new progress on the common basis of service to socialism.

The current situation, both international and domestic, is very favourable to the great cause of the reunification of our country. The Chinese Government has clearly proclaimed the general principles concerning Taiwan's return to the motherland. The CPPCC should take an active part in promoting the patriotic united front and working for Taiwan's early return, so as to accomplish national reunification. At the same time, it should actively expand people-to-people diplomacy, promote amicable exchanges with foreign friends and make its contribution to the growth of the international united front against aggression and expansionism.

In this new historical period, the CPPCC has a glorious task to fulfil, and it can do a great deal in its capacity as a united front organization. Let us unite under the banner of Marxism–Leninism and Mao Zedong Thought and, led by the Central Committee of the Communist Party, march forward along the socialist road towards the magnificent goal of the four modernizations.

May this session enjoy complete success!

Speech Greeting the Fourth Congress of Chinese Writers and Artists
30 October 1979

Delegates and Comrades,

Today, delegates representing our writers, dramatists, artists, musicians, performing artists, motion picture personnel and other workers in literature and art are gathered here to sum up their basic experience over the past thirty years and to discuss ways of building on their successes, overcoming shortcomings and thus making literature and art flourish in the new historical period. This is a happy and historic occasion and on behalf of the Central Committee of the Chinese Communist Party and the State Council, I am pleased to greet you warmly.

Taking part in this congress are veteran writers and artists who participated in the new cultural movement at the time of the May 4th Movement (1919), others who contributed to the cause of the people's liberation during later revolutionary periods, others who grew up after the founding of the People's Republic (1949), and still others who emerged in the struggle against Lin Biao and the Gang of Four. Also present are writers and artists from among our compatriots in Taiwan, Xianggang (Hongkong) and Aomen (Macao). This congress reflects the unprecedented unity of writers and artists throughout the country.

In the seventeen years before the Cultural Revolution, our line in literature and art was in the main correct and there were remarkable achievements. The allegation that our literature and art were then under the "dictatorship by the proponents of a sinister line" was nothing but slander on the part of Lin Biao and the Gang of Four. During the ten years when they ran riot, many outstanding works were proscribed, and many writers and artists framed and persecuted. A great number of our comrades and friends in literary and art circles resisted or fought against Lin Baio and the Gang with dignity and honour. Our writers and artists made admirable, lasting contributions in the struggle of the Party and the people to overthrow Lin Biao and the Gang. I salute them all.

Since the Gang was smashed, the Party's policy concerning intellectuals has been implemented in literary and art circles under the guidance of the Central Committee of the Party. A great many literary and art works that were popular in the past are once more available to the public. Writers and artists, with their minds at ease, are again enthusiastic and creative. In the few years since the criticism of the crimes and absurdities of Lin Biao and the Gang, many excellent novels, poems, plays, films, works of balladry, reportage pieces, musical compositions, dances, photographs and works of fine art have been produced. They have helped to break the mental shackles imposed by Lin Biao and the Gang and to eliminate their pernicious influence. They have helped to emancipate people's thinking, stimulate their enthusiasm and inspire them to march towards the goal of the four modernizations with one heart and one mind. Looking back over the last three years, I think that our writers and artists, like workers in other fields, have scored considerable achievements. They should enjoy the respect, trust and love of our Party and people. Through the ordeal of struggle, by and large our writers and artists have proved good, and the Party and people rejoice in this.

Delegates and Comrades,

Our country has entered a new period, a period of socialist modernization. Alongside the expansion of our productive forces, we should also reform and improve our socialist economic and political structures, build a highly-developed socialist democracy and perfect the socialist legal system. While working for a socialist civilization which is materially advanced, we should build one which is culturally and ideologically advanced by raising the scientific and cultural level of the whole nation and promoting a rich and diversified cultural life inspired by high ideals.

The overriding nationwide task for a considerable time to come will be to work single-mindedly for the four modernizations. This is a great enterprise which will determine our country's destiny for generations to come. The masses and cadres in all fields of endeavour should promote the emancipation of the mind, foster stability and unity, support the reunification of the motherland, and strive for the four modernizations. The basic standard for judging all our work is whether it helps or hinders our effort to modernize. The writers and artists, together with the educators, theorists, journalists, political workers and other comrades concerned, should carry out a protracted and effective struggle in the ideological sphere against all ideas and habits that obstruct the four modernizations. They should criticize the ideology of the exploiting classes and the conservative, narrow-minded mentality characteristic of small producers, criticize anarchism and ultra-individualism, and overcome bureaucracy. They should revive and carry forward the revolutionary traditions of our Party and people, cultivate fine morals and customs, and contribute to the building of a socialist civilization with a high cultural and ideological level.

In the pursuit of this noble cause, writers and artists find broad prospects opening before them. They are assuming important tasks, which they alone can perform, in order to meet the people's varied cultural needs, help bring up a new socialist generation, and raise the ideological, cultural and moral levels of our society.

Our literature and art belong to the people. Our people are hardworking, brave, indomitable and resourceful, and full of ideals. They love the motherland and socialism. They have the interests of the whole nation at heart and their sense of discipline is strong. For thousands of years, and especially in the half-century since the May 4th Movement, they have struggled arduously and confidently, overcoming all obstacles in their way and writing many brilliant chapters in our annals. No enemy, however strong, has subdued them and no difficulties, however great, have stopped their advance. Our literary and artistic creations must give expression to our people's outstanding qualities and celebrate their triumphs in revolution, in construction and in struggles against all kinds of enemies and hardships.

Our writers and artists should try harder to portray and help foster the new socialist man and achieve greater successes in doing so. We must portray the new features of the pioneers in the modernization drive, their revolutionary ideals and scientific approach, their lofty sentiments and creative ability, and their broad and realistic vision. Through images of this new man, we must stimulate the enthusiasm of the masses for socialism and inspire their creative activities, which are of historic significance in the pursuit of the four modernizations.

Our socialist writers and artists should create vivid, inspiring flesh-and-blood characters. Through them they should truthfully depict our rich social life and the inner qualities of our people as shown in their social relations, and give expression to the trend of historical development and to the demands of our progressive era. They should endeavour to educate the people in socialist ideology and imbue them with the drive and spirit necessary to build national strength and prosperity.

China has a long history, a vast territory, and a huge population. Our people are of many nationalities and of different professions, ages, experience and educational levels, and they have varied customs and cultural traditions and varied preferences in literature and art. All creative works—whether epic or cameo, serious or humorous, lyrical or philosophical—should have their place in our garden of literature and art, so long as they help to educate and enlighten the people while providing them with entertainment and aesthetic pleasure. The deeds of heroes, the labour, struggles, joys and sorrows, partings and reunions of ordinary people, and the life of our contemporaries and of our predecessors—all these should be depicted in our works of literature and art. We should draw on and learn from all that is progressive and advanced in the literature, art and performing arts of old China, and of other countries as well.

We must adhere to the principle put forward by Comrade Mao Zedong—that literature and art should serve the broadest masses and, first of all, the workers, peasants and soldiers. We must always uphold the principles of "letting a hundred flowers bloom", "weeding through the old to bring forth the new" and "making the past serve the present and foreign things serve China". We should encourage the unhampered development of different forms and styles in literature and art, as well as the free discussion of theories of literature and art among exponents of different views and schools of thought. Lenin once said that in literature "greater scope must undoubtedly be allowed for personal initiative, individual inclination, thought and fantasy, form and content". With the four modernizations as our common objective, the road before literature and art should become broader and broader. Guided by the correct principles for creative work, writers and artists should deal with an ever wider range of themes, increasingly vary their means of expression, and dare to blaze new trails. We must guard against or overcome the tendency to be formulistic and abstract, which produces monotonous, stiff, mechanical and stereotyped works.

Writers and artists who are responsible to the people should always keep their faces turned towards the masses and constantly improve their skills, doing their best to avoid slipshod work, seriously considering the likely impact of their works on society and trying to provide the people with the best mental nourishment. Lin Biao and the Gang of Four corrupted people's minds and poisoned the social atmosphere with reactionary and decadent exploiting-class ideology. Our revolutionary traditions and fine customs were seriously undermined as a result. Our writers and artists should use their creative works to broaden the people's mental horizons, and continue to fight resolutely against the pernicious influence of Lin Biao and the Gang. They should remain clear-headed when confronted by the proponents of erroneous tendencies, whether from the "Left" or from the Right, who are always attempting by one way or another to create disturbances and sabotage stability and unity, against the interests and wishes of the overwhelming majority of the people. Through literary and artistic creation and in close co-ordination with other ideological workers, they should help to raise the people's consciousness, make them understand the harmfulness of these erroneous tendencies and arouse strong public opinion against them, so that all society will unite to condemn and oppose them.

Writers and artists should conscientiously study Marxism–Leninism and Mao Zedong Thought so as to enhance their own ability to understand and analyse life and to see through appearances to the essence. We hope that more and more comrades in their ranks will become real "engineers of the human soul". In order to educate the people, one must first be educated himself; in order to give nourishment to the people, one must first absorb nourishment himself. And who is to educate and nourish our writers and artists? According to Marxism, the answer can only be: the people. It is the people who nurture our writers and artists. The creative life of all progressive writers and artists is rooted in their intimate ties with the people. Creativity withers when these ties are forgotten, neglected or severed. The people need art, but art needs the people even more. Writers and artists should consciously draw source material, themes, plots, language and poetic and artistic inspiration from the life of the people and be nourished by the dynamic spirit of the people, who make history. Fundamentally, this is the road which our socialist literature and art must take if it is to flourish. We believe that our writers and artists will march forward along this road steadily and unswervingly.

Writers and artists also need to constantly improve their professional skills. They should earnestly study, assimilate and expand upon all that is best in the literary and artistic techniques of every land and every age and perfect art forms with the distinctive features of our own nation and our own time. Only those writers and artists who defy difficulties, who study and practise diligently, and who dare to explore new ground can scale the artistic heights.

We sincerely hope that our writers and artists will unite more closely and expand their ranks. Whether professional or amateur, all socialist and patriotic writers and artists and all those who support the reunification of our motherland should try harder to help and learn from each other and to concentrate their energies on literary and artistic creation, study and criticism. It is for the people to judge the ideological and artistic value of a work. Listening with an open mind to criticism from different quarters and accepting useful advice are the key to constant progress and improvement. In literary and art circles we should encourage comradely, friendly discussions in which facts are presented and things are reasoned out. Such discussions should take place between creators who belong to different schools or work in different forms, between creators and critics, and between creators and their audiences. In the process, both criticism and counter-criticism should be permitted, the truth should be upheld and mistakes corrected.

Writers and artists of the older generation bear an important responsibility for discovering and training young people of talent. Our young writers and artists are vigorous and perceptive and in them lies the future of our literature and art. We should help them eagerly and also make strict demands on them, so that they will not become divorced from life but will make steady progress both ideologically and in their art. As for the middle-aged generation, they are the mainstay of our literary and art work, and we should make it possible for them to contribute all they can.

Special stress must be laid on the training of talented writers and artists. For a country as big as ours, with a population of over 900 million, we really have too few who are outstanding. This is quite out of keeping with the demands of our times. Through improved ideological and administrative work, we should create the necessary conditions for persons of outstanding talent to emerge and mature.

Party committees at all levels should give good leadership to literary and art work. Leadership doesn't mean handing out administrative orders and demanding that literature and art serve immediate, short-range political goals. It means understanding the special characteristics of literature and art and the laws of their development and creating conditions for them to flourish. That is, it means creating conditions that help writers and artists to improve their skills and to produce fine works and performances truly worthy of our great people and era. At present, it is particularly important to help writers and artists to continue emancipating their minds, to break the mental shackles fastened on them by Lin Biao and the Gang of Four and to keep to the correct political orientation. We must do everything—including providing appropriate material conditions—to ensure that our writers and artists can give full expression to their insight and talent. We maintain that leaders should exchange views with them as equals, and that those among them who are Party members should set an example through their own creations and unite with their non-Party colleagues so that all can advance together. The bureaucratic style of work must be dropped. There must be no more issuing of administrative orders regarding the creation and criticism of literature and art. To think that such a practice upholds Party leadership can only produce results opposite to those intended. It is essential to adhere to the ideological line of dialectical materialism, and to analyse both positive and negative experience in the development of our literature and art over the past thirty years. We must get rid of all stereotypes and conventions and study new situations and solve new problems in conformity with the characteristics of the new historical period China is in. The preposterous ways of Lin Biao and the Gang of Four undermined the Party's leadership in literature and art and destroyed their vitality. In the production of literature and art, which involves complex mental labour, it is essential that writers and artists follow their own creative spirit. What subjects they should choose for their creative work and how they should deal with those subjects are questions that writers and artists themselves must examine and gradually resolve through practice. There should be no arbitrary meddling in this process.

Delegates and Comrades,

At the time of the founding of our People's Republic, Comrade Mao Zedong pointed out that "an upsurge in economic construction is bound to be followed by an upsurge of construction in the cultural sphere". After waging bitter struggles and overcoming many difficulties, we have smashed the Gang of Four and thus removed our biggest stumbling block. We can now say with full assurance that this upsurge will not take long to appear and that the conditions are daily ripening that will enable us genuinely to put into practice the Marxist policy of "letting a hundred flowers bloom, a hundred schools of thought contend". Thanks to the hard work of the masses of writers and artists, a new period of flourishing literature and art will unfold before us.

The present congress is the first gathering of writers and artists from all over the country in this period of our new Long March. You comrades have been invited to it on the strength of your already considerable successes. We are sure that after the congress you will produce more and better works of literature and art to offer to the motherland and the people.

I wish this congress complete success!

Opening Speech at the Twelfth National Congress of the CPC
1 September 1982

Comrades,

I now declare the Twelfth National Congress of the Communist Party of China open.

There are three main tasks on our agenda: (1) to consider the report of the Eleventh Central Committee and decide on the Party's programme for opening up new prospects in all fields of socialist modernization; (2) to consider and adopt the new Constitution of the Communist Party of China; and (3) to elect a new Central Committee, a Central Advisory Commission and a Central Commission for Discipline Inspection, each according to the provisions of the new Party Constitution.

When these tasks have been accomplished, our Party will have clearer ideological guidelines for socialist modernization, our Party building will conform more closely to the needs of the new historical period, old and new cadres will be able to co-operate and new cadres will be able to succeed the old in the Party's highest leading organs, thus making the latter more vigorous and more militant.

A review of the Party's history will reveal this congress to be one of the most important since our Seventh National Congress.

The Seventh Congress, held in 1945 under Comrade Mao Zedong's chairmanship, was the most important after the founding of our Party in the period of democratic revolution. The delegates summed up the historical experience gained in the tortuous development of that revolution during the preceding quarter of a century, formulated a correct programme and correct tactics and overcame the wrong ideas inside the Party. They thus achieved unity of understanding based on Marxism–Leninism and Mao Zedong Thought. As a result, the Party itself became more united than ever before. It was the Seventh Congress that laid the foundation for the nationwide victory of the new-democratic revolution.

The Eighth Congress of the Party in 1956 analysed the situation following the basic completion of the socialist transformation of private ownership of the means of production and set the nation the task of all-round socialist construction. Its line was correct. However, because the Party was still inadequately prepared ideologically for all-round socialist construction, that line and the many correct views put forward at the congress were not persistently followed in practice. After the Eighth Congress, we suffered serious setbacks, although we also achieved many successes in socialist construction.

The present congress is being held in circumstances vastly different from those prevailing at the time of the Eighth Congress. Just as the quarter century of tortuous development of our democratic revolution before the Seventh Congress taught the Party to understand the laws governing that revolution, so the quarter-century of tortuous development of our socialist revolution and construction since the Eighth Congress has taught the Party profound lessons. Since the Third Plenary Session of the Eleventh Central Committee (December 1978), the Party has returned to its correct policies in the economic, political, cultural and other fields and in addition, after a study of the new situation and new experience, it has adopted a series of correct new policies. In comparison with the time of the Eighth Congress, our Party today has attained a much deeper understanding of the laws governing China's soicalist construction, acquired much more experience and become much more conscious and determined in implementing correct principles. We have every reason to believe that the correct programme that will be decided on at this congress will create a new situation in all fields of socialist modernization and bring prosperity to our Party, our socialist cause, our country and the people of all our nationalities.

In carrying out our modernization programme we must proceed from Chinese realities. Both in revolution and construction, we should also learn from foreign countries and draw on their experience. But the mechanical copying and application of foreign experience and models will get us nowhere. We have had many lessons in this respect. We must integrate the universal truth of Marxism with the concrete realities of China, blaze a path of our own and build a socialism with Chinese characteristics—that is the basic conclusion we have reached after summing up long historical experience.

China's affairs should be run in the light of China's specific conditions and by the Chinese people themselves. Independence and self-reliance have always been and will always be our basic stand. While we Chinese people value our friendship and co-operation with other countries and other peoples, we value even more our hard-won independence and sovereign rights. No foreign country can expect China to be its vassal nor can it expect China to accept anything harmful to China's interests. We will unswervingly follow a policy of opening to the outside world and actively increase exchanges with foreign countries on the basis of equality and mutual benefit. At the same time, we will keep clear heads, firmly resist corrosion by decadent ideas from abroad and never permit the bourgeois way of life to spread in our country. We, the Chinese people, have our national self-respect and pride. We deem it the highest honour to love our socialist motherland and contribute our all to her socialist construction. We deem it the deepest disgrace to impair her interests, dignity and honour.

The 1980s will be an important decade in the history of our Party and state. To step up socialist modernization, to strive for China's reunification and particularly for the return of Taiwan to the motherland, and to oppose hegemonism and work to safeguard world peace—these are the three major tasks of our people in the 1980s. Economic construction is at the core of these tasks; it is the basis for the solution of our external and internal problems. For a long time to come, at least for the eighteen years until the end of the century, we must bend every effort to do the following four things: restructure the administration and the economy and make our cadre ranks more revolutionary, younger in average age, better educated and professionally more competent; strive to build a socialist civilization which is culturally and ideologically advanced; combat economic and other crimes that undermine socialism; and rectify the Party's style of work and consolidate its organization on the basis of a conscientious study of the new Party Constitution. These will be the most important guarantees that we keep to the socialist road and concentrate our efforts on modernization.

Ours is now a large Party with 39 million members that leads the whole people in the exercise of state power. However, the Communist Party will always be a minority in the population as a whole. None of the major tasks proposed by the Party can be accomplished without the hard work of the masses. Here, on behalf of the Party, I wish to pay high tribute to all workers, peasants and intellectuals who have toiled diligently for socialist modernization, and to the People's Liberation Army—that Great Wall of steel safeguarding the security and socialist construction of our motherland.

China's democratic parties fought together with our Party in the period of the democratic revolution, and together with us they have advanced and undergone tests in the socialist period. In the construction work ahead, our Party will continue its long-term co-operation with all patriotic democratic parties and patriotic democrats. On our Party's behalf, I wish to express sincere gratitude to all the democratic parties and to all our friends without party affiliation.

The cause of our Party has enjoyed the support and assistance of progressive people and friendly countries throughout the world. On behalf of our Party, I wish to express our sincere thanks to them.

We must do our work carefully and well. We must strengthen our Party's unity with the people of all nationalities in our country and with the people of the world. We must struggle hard to make China a modern socialist country that is highly democratic and culturally advanced. We must also oppose hegemonism, work to safeguard world peace and promote human progress.

Speech delivered at the National Day Ceremony
1 October 1984

Comrade Officers and Men of the PLA,
Fellow Countrymen, Comrades and Friends,
   On this glorious day of the thirty-fifth anniversary of the founding of the great People's Republic of China, I extend the warmest festive greetings to comrades, fellow countrymen and friends who are working for socialist modernization, national reunification and the defence of the motherland.
   Thirty-five years ago Chairman Mao Zedong, great leader of the people of all our nationalities, solemnly proclaimed here the founding of the People's Republic of China and declared that the Chinese people had stood up. In the past thirty-five years in China, not only was the past dark period of history wholly terminated but a socialist society built up, and this has changed the course of human history. Particularly after the Third Plenary Session of the Eleventh Central Committee of the CPC, the perverse acts of the counter-revolutionary Gang of Four were thoroughly redressed, the method of thinking advocated by Comrade Mao Zedong and characterized by seeking truth from facts was restored and developed, and a number of important policies suited to the new situation have been adopted. Thus the whole country has taken on a new look. On the basis of national stability, unity, democracy and rule of law, we have placed socialist modernization above everything else in our work. Our economy has developed more vigorously than ever before, and achievements in all other fields are widely acknowledged. Today, all our people are full of joy and pride.
   The Party's Twelfth National Congress set the target of quadrupling, by the year of 2000, the annual gross value of industrial and agricultural output of 1980. Developments in the past few years show that this magnificent target can be reached. Our primary job at present is to reform systematically whatever is impeding our progress in the existing economic structures. At the same time, we shall carry out planned technical transformation of existing enterprises throughout the country and greatly strengthen our scientific-technological research, school education at all

levels and the training of all workers, functionaries and cadres. The whole Party and the whole society must truly value knowledge and let intellectuals play their role. All this will enable us gradually to realize our modernization programme.

China's foreign policy is known to all, and it will remain unchanged. We stand firmly for the maintenance of world peace, for the relaxation of international tension and for the reduction of armaments, first of all the nuclear and other armaments of the superpowers, and we are opposed to all aggression and hegemonism. China will remain open to the outside world, and is ready to establish and develop diplomatic relations and economic and cultural ties with all countries on the basis of the Five Principles of Peaceful Coexistence. We stand for the settlement of international disputes through negotiations, just as we have settled the question of Hongkong with the United Kingdom through negotiations. In the seriously deteriorating international situation, we must strengthen our national defence. All officers and men of the Chinese People's Liberation Army must be alert at all times, constantly improve their military and political qualities and strive to gain knowledge and ability for modern warfare.

We stand for the peaceful reunification with Taiwan, which is part of our sacred territory. Our policy in this regard is also known to all and will not change. It is being rooted in the hearts of all descendants of the Yellow Emperor. Being an irresistible trend, the peaceful reunification of our motherland will sooner or later come true. We hope that the people of all our nationalities, including all compatriots in Hongkong, Macao, Taiwan and those residing abroad, will work together for its early realization.

Long live the great People's Republic of China!

Long live the great Communist Party of China!

Long live the great People's Liberation Army of China!

Long live the great unity of the people of all nationalities of China!

Interview of Deng Xiaoping by Robert Maxwell on Current Affairs

Question: The Chinese Government has stated that the normalization of Sino-American relations reflects the Chinese view that "question of strategy" is involved. Does that imply that China looks ahead to a strategic relationship with the U.S.A.? Now if that were to be the case, how would that consideration affect China's position in the third world?

Answer: The significance of the normalization of Sino-U.S. relations is certainly not confined to the relations between the two countries. The maintenance of normal relations between China and the United States is not only in the fundamental interests of the two peoples, but conducive to peace and stability in Asia and the world as a whole. However, these relations can only be based on mutual respect for sovereignty and non-interference in each other's internal affairs, that is, on the U.S. Government's termination of its arms sales to Taiwan and its policy to create "two Chinas" or "one China, one Taiwan".

China belongs to the Third World. We have always based our foreign policy on our unity and co-operation with other Third World countries. Our foreign policy is: Stand firmly on the side of the Third World countries and unite with all the forces that can be united to oppose hegemonism of any kind and maintain world peace.

Question: In the course of normalization of relations between China and the United States, you knew that the U.S. Congress was going to pass the "Taiwan Relations Act". So was not the supply of American arms to Taiwan clearly foreseeable? If this issue is not resolved, Sino-American relations will reverse. What would be the implication of such a reversal if it comes to that?

Answer: The U.S. arms sales to Taiwan constitute an act of infringement on China's sovereignty and interference in China's internal affairs. Shortly after the establishment of Sino-U.S. diplomatic relations, the U.S. Congress, in disregard of norms governing international relations and in violation of the principles embodied in the joint communiqué on the establishment of diplomatic relations between the two countries, passed the so-called "Taiwan Relations Act". The Chinese Government immediately lodged a strong protest with the U.S. side. In the past three years since the establishment of diplomatic relations, we have repeatedly stated our solemn position against U.S. arms sales to Taiwan. There is no room for bargaining on the question of safeguarding China's sovereignty.

Question: What are the concrete obstacles to the normalization of China's relations with the U.S.S.R.? Is the crux of the problem in the field of state relations, in the border dispute?

Answer: We have always stood for maintaining and developing state relations with all countries, including the Soviet Union, on the basis of the Five Principles of Peaceful Co-existence. However, there are indeed many obstacles in the way of improving Sino-Soviet relations, the biggest being Soviet persistence in pursuing a hegemonist foreign policy.

The Soviet leaders talked about improving Sino-Soviet relations in the past, too. And recently in Tashkent, President Brezhnev again spoke of Sino-Soviet relations and expressed his intention to improve these relations. We have taken note of this, but we have also noted his attack on China's position in the same speech. What we attach importance to are concrete actions of the Soviet Union in our bilateral relations and in international affairs, first of all, of course, actions on questions concerning the Sino-Soviet boundary and Soviet troop withdrawal from the border and also questions of Afghanistan, Viet Nam and Indo-China, etc.

Question: What role do you see China playing in the contradictory relationship between North and South, with regard to the economic question?

Answer: Since the beginning of the 1980s, the international situation has become more turbulent. The need to improve North–South economic relations and establish a just and equitable new international economic order has become all the more pressing. We hope that the developed countries will follow the trend of the times and adopt wise policies on this issue.

The process of establishing a new international economic order implies, among other things, the strengthening of what is known as South–South co-operation. We Third World countries shall mainly rely on co-operation among ourselves. Each and every Third World country has its own characteristics and strong points, and so there are broad areas where they can co-operate. China will work together with other Third World countries in an effort to establish the new international economic order and promote South–South co-operation.

Question: May I ask you to give your views on the prospects for

Sino-Vietnamese relations in the light of the continuing problem of Kampuchea?

Answer: China and Viet Nam used to enjoy very friendly relations. We on our part haven't done anything to Viet Nam which we need to feel sorry about. The root cause for the deterioration of Sino-Vietnamese relations lies in the pursuance by the Vietnamese authorities of a policy of regional hegemony in an attempt to set up a so-called "Greater Indochinese federation" and in their taking China as an insurmountable obstacle to the realization of their ambition for regional hegemony. Hence their wanton anti-China activities.

Even to this day, the Vietnamese authorities have refused to comply with the U.N. resolutions calling for their troop withdrawal from Kampuchea, and instead they are continuing to intensify their war of aggression against Kampuchea, thus further threatening the peace and security of Thailand and Southeast Asia as a whole. Moreover, the Vietnamese authorities have written into their Constitution opposition to China as their state policy, which was reaffirmed not long ago at the Fifth National Congress of their Party. Therefore, in exploring the prospects of improved Sino-Vietnamese relations, one must try to find out, first of all, whether the Vietnamese authorities have any sincere desire to change their position and policy. There are no obstacles from the Chinese side.

Question: What is your estimation of the popular movement against nuclear armaments and for peace?

Answer: The opposition by the masses in the Western countries to the Soviet–U.S. arms race and to nuclear war and their concern for peace are legitimate and reasonable. We deeply sympathize with them and believe that their endeavour will contribute positively to the cause of maintaining world peace.

Question: We are sometimes confused in the West about what the present domestic political situation in China actually is. On the one hand, we read reassurance that the basic situation is one of stability and order. But on the other there are reports of a "crisis of confidence" in the establishment—particularly of public confidence in the Chinese Communist Party. Can you give me a balanced view of all this?

Answer: The present political situation in China is so stable as is rarely seen in the past two decades or more. The income of the peasants has increased substantially thanks to appropriate agricultural policies. The urban staff and workers are happy, too, as their real income has gone up, more family members are employed, and their housing conditions have improved. These are the facts. So, in China today, there is no such thing as "crisis of public confidence in the establishment". However, there are a few young people who had no access to good education and whose families including themselves suffered various misfortunes during the "cultural revolution". As a result of this grave political chaos, they are puzzled over many questions for the time being. That is hardly avoidable. But facts are most convincing. These young people will start making progress afresh after they have pondered over the matter seriously. Now again, there have emerged many young people who take pleasure in helping others and work selflessly. Stories about them are very moving indeed.

Question: More than five years after Mao Zedong's death, far-reaching changes continue to take place in almost every sphere of Chinese life. What has been the purpose of introducing these major changes and are they, in your opinion, proving successful?

Answer: Far-reaching changes are indeed taking place in every sphere of life in Chinese society. The mistakes of the "cultural revolution" must be liquidated and other practices which have proved irrational over the years must also be rectified. The various reforms carried out in recently years are all strictly socialist-oriented; they fall in line with the basic ideological principles long upheld by the late Chairman Mao Zedong and have yielded marked results. I believe that China will make still greater progress in the future.

Question: Since 1978 we have seen the introduction of major reforms in both the policies and the structure of the Chinese economy. What might these reforms necessitate and what do you expect them to achieve?

Answer: In the past we carried out socialist transformation of the private ownership of the means of production and established socialist public ownership, thus ensuring the growth of our economy. However, there were quite a few defects in our economic management system due to lack of experience. They are mainly manifested in over-centralized management power, over-rigid control and egalitarianism in distribution.

In our reforms, on the premise of persisting in the planned economy, we have delegated greater power to the local administrations and enterprises and given scope to the supplementary role of regulation through the market. With regard to the structure of ownership, the state and collective sectors remain the basic forms in China's economy. The individual economy of urban and rural working people operating within certain prescribed limits and under state control is a necessary complement to the public sector of the economy. Experience has proved that this helps to make up for the inadequacies of the state and collective economies, create more job opportunities and revitalize socio-economic life. But the state will not permit any activities in the individual sector of the economy to undermine the socialist economy.

Question: Eighty per cent of the Chinese people live in the countryside and farm the land; they have to feed themselves, feed the cities and as well provide a surplus to the state for the development of the economy. In the past we in the West looking at China have come to believe that those objectives were best served by collectivized agriculture based on the people's communes, but now I understand that the communes are being dismantled, that production decisions are reverting to households, families and sometimes even individuals. Can you explain what has led your Government to conclude that this fundamental change of policy of the agricultural economy is necessary? Do you think there is a possibility that the reforms we have discussed might lead on to private ownership of the means of production, including even the land?

Answer: The people's commune practises a system of three-level ownership, namely, by the commune, the production brigade and the production team, with the production team as the basic accounting unit. Now in the main, we still adhere to this system in the countryside. The Draft of the "Revised Constitution of the People's Republic of China" published recently embodies the principle of separating government administration from commune management in the countryside by re-instituting the township administration while keeping the people's commune as a collective economic organization, so that each may give full scope to its own functions. The dismantling of people's communes is out of the question. In the past few years, we have introduced multiple forms of the system of job responsibility for agricultural production within the framework of the people's communes, mainly involving changes in the previous ways of management and administration. These changes are aimed at bringing the initiative of the peasants into fuller play and giving them more decision-making power in both production and management, so as to overcome the drawbacks of egalitarianism which have long existed in the collective economy. True, private ownership of some means of production, such as farm cattle and small farm implements, is now permissible. There is nothing wrong with it. But private ownership is impermissible with regard to the land, water conservancy facilities, important means of production, industrial enterprises and other large-scale side-line occupations run by the commune, production brigade or team. Therefore, our rural economy is still a collective economy of the working people, and not the kind of individual economy of private ownership as prevailed before the co-operative movement. For the sake of more effective production and management, the peasants have started various new forms of associations. Of course, in a few localities poor work has caused damage to the collective property and the authority of collective organizations. However, this deviation is being corrected.

Question: Can one assume that the size of the ministries and organs of the State Council has been reduced to a more realistic level?

Answer: Yes. But this is just the beginning of streamlining the administrative structure. Other reforms are still going on, with a view to defining clearly the functions and responsibilities of each and every organ or individual, raising efficiency and making every functionary qualified for his post.

Question: China's political energy in 1982 is being spent in a major drive against bureaucracy, corruption, political recalcitrance of the Party and the Government top cadres. How is the drive going and for how long will it continue?

Answer: No such problem as "political recalcitrance" in its general sense has ever existed in the central organs of the Party and government or among the top Party and government cadres since the collapse of the Lin Biao and Jiang Qing counter-revolutionary cliques in China.

As to the bureaucracy and corruption which you have mentioned, they are indeed impermissible in a socialist country. We are determined to combat such phenomena as long as they exist.

Question: The policy with which you are personally associated is that of boosting consumer goods output at the expense of heavy industry. Is it likely to continue in the foreseeable future?

The emphasis your Government has placed upon the needs to raise the standard of living of the Chinese people has necessitated the expansion of the consumer goods industries which I understand must have been at the cost of some reduction in spending on investment and construction. Are there dangers in this of growing dependence on imported manufactures? And I have read that the returning of production choices to lower levels and even households has resulted in a switch to cash crops. Might that not simultaneously prolong dependence on more grain imports?

Answer: No one individual in the present Chinese leadership can determine any of our policies on his own. All important decisions are made through collective discussions.

To raise the people's living standards is a long-term task which will certainly be carried on for years to come. However, in the final analysis, the improvement of the people's livelihood depends on increased production, including that of agriculture, consumer and heavy industries. Appropriate proportions will be set for their development in our economic plans to prevent growing dependence on imports. In agriculture, while developing cash crops, we will see to it that there is no drop in the production of food grains.

Question: My reading about China's development strategy up to the mid-1970s suggested that great emphasis was placed on fundamental social problems, summed up in what you used to call "closing the three great difficulties" or "gaps" (town/country, worker/peasant, manual/mental labour). Do you see current policies as still serving that objective?

Answer: The emphasis of our development strategy is still placed on the solution of fundamental social problems. As for closing the gaps between town and country, worker and peasant, manual and mental labour, this is an ideal which will be realized gradually over a very long period of time. Overhastiness will only cause damage to economic development.

Question: Your Government is now placing very great emphasis on the need to limit population growth, and I fully understand the demographic importance behind that policy, but I remember when the Indian Government put into effect a very rigorous policy with the same objective that became sometimes coercive coupled with economic inducements that led to a very strong backlash in public feeling, which, in the long run, set back the whole family planning programme. Do you think there might be a danger that your own "one child family" programme could run into similar difficulties, especially of course, in the countryside?

Answer: Since the beginning of the 1970s when China made family planning and lower population growth rate a strategic task, it has carried out extensive education coupled with the necessary administrative measures to limit population growth and raise the population quality. We encourage each couple to have one child only and have achieved marked results in the cities. In the rural areas, however, it is necessary to do more work of persuasion among the peasants, and limited concessions are allowed for those who have real problems.

Question: As is well known, shortage of energy is a crucial factor in China's problems. What are the plans to overcome this?

Answer: Generally speaking, China is not short of energy resources. The main problem is insufficient extraction and huge waste in their use. Besides, energy resources are unevenly distributed over the country, so transport facilities have to be improved greatly. Efforts are now being concentrated on solving these problems.

Question: To what extent will China's economic development be based on open-door policy—or to put it another way, what is the essential balance between the traditional policy of self-reliance and the new policy of the open door?

China's "open door" policy to encourage foreign investment is now in its fourth year. Are you satisfied with the progress this policy is making, and what would you say to the readers of this interview who are interested in making investment in China by way of encouraging them to do so?

Answer: The policy of self-reliance was carried out during the revolutionary wars and must be adhered to in economic development after the founding of new China as well. It is impossible for a big country like China to live on borrowed money or achieve growth by imitating others.

However, China does not intend to take a self-sufficient and self-seclusive approach. We should make the best use of the advanced experience, technology and funds of foreign countries to accelerate our economic development.

We have achieved some successes in our policy of opening to the outside world. Foreign businessmen willing to do business with or make investment in China on the basis of the principle of equality and mutual benefit are all welcome to do so.

Index

Academic exchanges, international 45
Administrative structure, streamlining of 96
Afghanistan 92
Agriculture 40, 44, 50
　cash crops 96
　communes 95
　co-operatives 2, 7, 29, 95
　private ownership in 95
　secondary schools of 59
　see also Peasants
Anti-Party alliance 23
Armaments
　international reduction of 90
　nuclear 93
Army 7, 17, 23, 30, 50, 62, 87, 89–90
Artists see under Writers

Bourgeois ideology in China 47, 55
Brezhnev, L. I. 92
Bureaucracy, tendencies towards 8–12, 96

Centralism, democratic 14–15, 18
Centralization, undue emphasis on 14
Chiang Kai-shek 1
　government of 2
Children's Corps 56
Communist Party of China ix, 93
　and state organs 22
　Central Committee 12–21, 23–29, 35, 38, 62, 64, 74, 86
　committee system 16–17
　conferences 18–19
　Congresses 11, 18–19
　　7th 1–4, 7, 18, 30, 33–34, 38, 85
　　8th 1, 18, 38, 85–86
　　11th 53, 85
　　12th 85, 89
　Constitution of see Constitution
　co-operation with non-Party people 11–12, 22
　disciplinary measures 33
　leadership in 15–17, 20, 51
　mass line of 4–12, 21, 28, 60
　membership of 2, 26–34, 36, 87
　organizations, functions and powers of 13–15, 35–37

Communist Party of Soviet Union (CPSU), 20th Congress 15, 21
Communist Youth League 35, 37, 56
Conferences, National
　Chinese People's Political Consultative Conference, 5th National Committee of 53, 75–77
　on Education 54–61
　on Financial and Economic Work 23–24
　on Organizational Work 23–24
　of Party Representatives 23, 37
　on the Question of Intellectuals 19
　on Science 40–53
　of Secretaries of Provincial and Municipal Party Committees 18
　on the State Monopoly of the Purchase and Marketing of Grain 18
　on the Transformation of Capitalist Industry and Commerce 19
Congresses
　4th Congress of Chinese Writers and Artists 78–84
　see also under Communist Party of China
Conscription 29
Constitution 18, 66, 68, 85
　revision of 1–39, 95
Corruption, drive against 96
Criticism and self-criticism 3, 14, 25, 28, 47
　rectification campaigns 25, 30
Cultural Revolution ix, 70, 94
Culture 78–84

Decentralism 13–14
Defence, national 40, 44
Democracy 65, 68

Economic construction 87
Economy, the 71, 73, 74, 94, 97
Education
　general 49, 54–61
　higher 55, 59
　ideological 55–56, 77
　political 55–56, 77
　teachers 60
　vocational/technical 59
Energy resources 97
Engels, Friedrich 58

Five-year plans
  First 1, 39
Food, production of 96
Foreign policy 90
Formalism 53

Gang of Four 40–41, 44–46, 48–49, 52, 54–56, 61, 63, 78–79, 81, 83, 89
Gao Gang 23

Health, public 8
Hongkong 76, 90

Ideological education 3, 55–56, 77
Individual, glorification of the 20–21
Indo-China 92
Industrialization, socialist 26
Industry 40, 50
  iron and steel 44
Intellectuals 29, 31, 40, 43–46, 54–55, 75, 78–79
  Conference on the Question of 19
  persecution of 44–46, 54
Inventions, Chinese 44
Investment, foreign 97–98

Japan 2, 11
  Japanese occupation 2
  War of Resistance against 11, 13, 49
Jiang Qing 40, 96

Kampuchea 93
Kuomintang 2, 7

Labour
  mental 44, 58
  power 42
  productivity 55
Legal system 68
Lenin, V. I. 20, 43, 54–55, 58, 72
Lin Biao 44, 46, 48, 78–79, 81, 83, 96
Liu Shaoqi 1, 4

Macao 76, 90
Mao Zedong ix, 1, 3, 5, 21, 31, 38, 43–44, 49, 52–53, 63, 65, 67, 70, 74, 76, 85, 89, 94
  and art and literature 71, 84
  and education 54, 56–57, 69–70
  and intellectuals 46–47
  Thoughts of 57, 60, 65, 69, 74, 77, 82
Marx, Karl 41, 43, 58
Marxism 5, 20, 52, 65
Masses, consultation/contact with the 5–10, 12, 14–15, 20
Media, the 72–73
Modernization programme 41, 44, 46, 52, 73–77, 79, 86–87

Nationalities in China 75–76
New international economic order 92

Peace movements, international 93
Peaceful coexistence, five principles of 90, 92
Peasants 29, 93–95
  and family planning 97
People's Liberation Army 7, 17, 23, 50, 87, 89–90
People's Revolution 21–22
Personality cult 15, 21
Population, limiting the growth of 97
Production 44, 50, 63
  means of 42
Proletarian internationalism 31

Rao Shushi 23
Responsibility, individual 17, 20, 50–51

Science and technology 40–53, 55
  backwardness in 45
  National Conference on Science 40–53
  research/institutes 50–51
Scientists and technicians 46–52
Socialist construction 85–87
Standard of living, raising the 96
State Council 74, 95–96

Taiwan 39, 76–77, 87, 90
  Taiwan Relations Act 91–92
  U.S. arms sales to 91–92
Thailand 93
Third World countries 91–92
Tiananmen Incident 66

United Kingdom 90
U.S.A.
  Sino-U.S. relations 91–92
  U.S. arms sales to Taiwan 91–92
U.S.S.R.
  CPSU, 20th Congress 15, 21
  Sino-Soviet relations 92

Viet Nam 92
  Sino-Vietnamese relations 93

Wang Hongwen 40
War of Liberation 7, 13, 30
War of Resistance against Japan 11, 13, 49
Women in the Party 31, 34
Writers and artists 78–84
  training of 83

Yao Wenyuan 40
Young Pioneers 56

Zhang Chunqiao 40